Bo... for Rent

Body for Rent

THE TERRIFYING TRUE STORY OF TWO ORDINARY
GIRLS SOLD FOR SEX AGAINST THEIR WILL

ANNA HENDRIKS
and OLIVIA SMIT

with TIM TATE

First published in 2019 by Trapeze,
an imprint of The Orion Publishing Group Ltd
Carmelite House, 50 Victoria Embankment,
London EC4Y 0DZ

An Hachette UK company

1 3 5 7 9 10 8 6 4 2

A CIP catalogue record for this book is
available from the British Library.

ISBN (Paperback): 978 1 4091 9274 9
ISBN (eBook): 978 1 4091 9275 6

Typeset by Born Group
Printed and bound in Great Britain by Clays Ltd, Elcograf S.p.A.

www.orionbooks.co.uk

Contents

Authors' Note

This is a true story.

We have, however, been forced to conceal our true identities: Anna Hendriks and Olivia Smit are not our real names. When we set out to write this book, we did not intend to adopt pseudonyms, but as we progressed, we came to understand the dangers this would entail, the pain our families would endure, and the damage to their lives and welfare once their employers and their communities heard about our story.

Using our own names posed a risk to us too. Prostitution may be legal in Holland and even celebrated for its apparent freedom and its contribution to the economy, but sex work – legal or otherwise, voluntary or enforced – carries an enduring stigma. We have learned, sometimes at great cost, that society all too often blames the victims of the sex trade, rather than the men (and it is almost always men) who exploit them.

Escaping from the sex trade was one of the hardest parts of our journey, and we realised that if we 'outed' ourselves as former prostitutes, we would never be more than one click of the mouse, one casual Google search, away from our past and the casual condemnation of what we once were; we would never truly be free of the Red Light District.

For all those reasons we reluctantly came to the conclusion that we could not use our real names or that of our exploiter. The price for doing so would be humiliation for our families, the disapproval of our current employers in the real world, and the lingering pity or condemnation of those who have never experienced what we endured.

From the beginning and throughout everything that happened, there were two of us; we were bound together by shared isolation and unhappiness, and made inseparable by each successive misstep or misfortune. For that reason, we have written (almost) alternating chapters, taking it in turn to tell each stage of our story.

Introduction

At 7 p.m. precisely we draw back the curtains of our glass prisons.

We stand, half dressed and dulled by alcohol, in the neon-lit windows of Amsterdam's Red Light District, ready to begin the night's work of selling our tired and bruised bodies to anyone with the price of entry.

Over the next nine hours, we will service the sexual demands of an average of eight customers each. Couples occasionally, but mainly men: young men and old men; normal family men – someone's fathers, uncles or brothers – as well as those whose pleasure runs to pain, degradation and torture.

Each encounter begins with the same repetitive mantra of our trade: 'Fifty euros – suck and fuck'. We lead the customers into our small, spartan rooms, take their money, close the curtains and begin the ritual of industrialised sex.

We sanitize their genitals with a chemical spray, roll a condom over their penis and take them – as briefly as possible – into our mouths. Then we adopt the position each client has chosen for the sex itself: missionary or doggy-style, never both. Additional positions, along with the removal of our bras, cost another €50.

Then we lie on the hard, joyless bed, motionless and silent, as each man takes his selfish pleasure inside us. While we wait for them to finish, we try to distance our minds from what is being done to our bodies; sending our thoughts to find refuge somewhere – anywhere – other than the place in which we work. The drink helps, but not always, and not enough.

No child dreams of this life. No little girl grows up with the hope of one day renting her body to dozens of men, night in, night out, allowing them to penetrate her, careless of the damage they cause. Yet for thousands – tens of thousands – of women, this is what happens. Six nights a week, we are two of them.

We do not fit the common stereotypes of prostitution. We are not drug addicts, nor – yet – fully dependent on alcohol. We were not sexually abused as children. We come from respectable middle-class families with comfortable homes in the suburbs. And yet within days of reaching the legal age to sell sex, we were forced to work behind the windows of the most famous Red Light District in the world.

It is April 2004. We have been trapped in our glass-fronted cubicles for more than three hundred nights. Already, we have serviced the sexual demands of hundreds of men. Our world – once happy and filled with hope – has shrunk to the dimensions of the bare rooms in which we sell ourselves.

We are eighteen years old and hardened prostitutes. How on earth did we get here?

This is the story of how we – two vulnerable young girls – fell or, more accurately, were groomed, into the brutal, multi-million-euro commercial sex trade. For more than seven and five years respectively, we worked in the neon-lit glass windows of Amsterdam's Red Light District, one of the world's most popular – and profitable – tourist attractions. Some of what we describe may shock you, but it is the truth about how the legalised prostitution industry works. Some of our actions may make you shake your heads or even despise us, for we made mistakes which contributed to our ordeal, but we hope you will try to understand why we behaved as we did. Because however shocking, however disturbing, this is a true story.

In theory – and in the tourist information distributed across the world – our workplace was a secure space; somewhere women chose willingly to rent their bodies for sex, safeguarded by law and protected by police from traffickers, pimps and violent clients. But this theory is a myth; a fantasy cynically sold by those who control, or profit from, the trade in women's bodies. We are the living proof that prostitution in the Red Light District is neither voluntary nor safe. We were coerced into sexual slavery by a brutal pimp who controlled every aspect of our lives.

We experienced the worst degradation human beings can inflict on one another, required to accommodate every extreme fetish harboured by the men who knocked on our windows.

We were so regularly abused by our pimp and so degraded by what he made us do that fear and numbness became our default state of being. Gradually, every aspect of the ordinary, middle-class girls we had once been leached away until there was nothing of us left.

We also came to understand the corruption, organised crime, violence and drug dealing that underpins the neon-lit streets of the Red Light District. We witnessed the plight of other young girls and women, many of them trafficked from overseas into this so-called legal industry by violent pimping gangs, and kept compliant with threats or drugs while the police turned a blind eye.

It took all the strength and resolve we possessed – and the enduring bonds of our childhood friendship – to pull ourselves out of the world in which we had existed for so long.

Few people know the reality of legalised prostitution. We do – and that is why we knew we had to write this book. To give girls like us – hidden from plain sight and exploited beyond endurance for the casual pleasure of anyone with the price of admission – a voice; to make you, the lucky ones who never fell into the clutches of the commercial sex trade, see how it trapped us. Above all, we want to prevent other young women falling into the traps that ensnared us. After all, this is a story that could have happened to any one of you, or to your family or friends. It *does* happen, every day, to normal, respectable girls; girls exactly like us, girls that we once were.

Once upon a time we were not really any different from most of you. Or your children. Or a young girl you know. And yet at the age of sixteen, we were groomed and then forced into the commercial sex industry.

This is the story of how it happened.

ONE

Anna: Once Upon a Time

A photograph. It is summer; a small, slight blonde girl smiles shyly at the camera, a moment of childhood innocence captured by the snap of a lens. It is 1996 and I am that child, playing in my garden, soaking up the afternoon sunshine, secure in the warmth of a close-knit, loving family.

Who was I then? I was you. Or your daughter. I looked no different from millions of other eleven-year-old girls the world over. I seemed happy. Yet in less than twelve months, my safe little world would shatter for ever, and the path towards where, in just five years' time, I would end up was set in stone.

So look closer at the photo, its colours fading faster than the memories it captured: is there something in it – a tilt of the head, a cast in my eyes – something, anything, to give a sign of what I would become? No. And then again, yes. If you look closely.

I was born in April 1985 in a small village on the outskirts of Amsterdam. My childhood home was in a row of well-built terraced houses, each with a large garden. There were three bedrooms and I was given the biggest one, right at the top of the house. I was an only child; my mother wanted to have a second baby and I always longed for a brother or sister, but my father refused to contemplate any more children – and I soon learned that in our house, his word was the law and final.

I never knew why he was so opposed to having a second child, but whatever the reason it certainly wasn't financial. My parents were solidly middle class and comfortably off. My father had a good office job, running the business affairs of a local housing association and my mother brought in extra money by working at a café. Although this sometimes involved evening shifts, my father was always home to take care of me before she had to leave the house.

Ours was a close-knit extended family, with three generations living in the same village. My maternal grandfather had a house close to ours, and my mother's brothers also lived nearby. My father's family was spread all over Holland, but we visited them every month or so. I was growing up in a happy, loving environment – and I never for one moment thought that this would change.

As a family we went everywhere, did everything, together: I was included in adult dinner parties, and although we never went on foreign holidays, we spent long, relaxed summers at the beach, with frequent day-trips to amusement parks. In truth, I was probably a bit spoiled; I loved sport and my parents indulged my passions. They took me to swimming and dance classes – both ballet and freestyle – and paid for horse-riding lessons and pony treks.

Academically, I flourished. I enjoyed going to my primary school and, secure in the love, support and encouragement of my family, I always achieved good grades and brought home glowing reports from my teachers.

Throughout those childhood years, I was very much a daddy's girl. He was always the one to take me shopping, to buy me clothes and whatever I needed for school. I knew that my mother loved me, but I spent more quality time with Father and felt emotionally closer to him. Although he was strict (it was always he who made me sit at the big dining-room table to do my homework, forcing me to stare at the textbooks until I finished, even though I cried), I felt we had a deep and unbreakable bond.

And we were a settled family. Unlike other children in the village, I don't recall ever hearing – much less witnessing – arguments or fights between my parents. They were always very affectionate towards each other, holding hands or curling up on the couch together; they kissed frequently and openly and they were, or so it seemed, very much in love. To my child's mind, they were – and I was – idyllically happy.

Looking back, though, I wonder about how happy I truly was. From very early in my childhood, I was extremely shy and I often felt uncomfortable if my family, or my teachers, made me the centre of attention. In part this was due to the way I looked: I was much taller than the other children in the village but at the same time I was extremely skinny; as puberty approached, I became very insecure about my body.

Nor did I have many friends. I was never the sort of child who enjoyed being part of a large group; I was only comfortable with having one close companion at a time – and I was also acutely aware that even this was one too many for my mother. I came to feel that she resented anyone I grew close to, and it gradually dawned on me that she was jealous: she wanted all my attention and begrudged me spending time with anyone else.

I think this was because of something my grandfather had been told by his father: he used to say that 'You only have one best girlfriend – and that's your mother.' This lesson was passed down, generation to generation, as a piece of unimpeachable family lore, and by the time I was old enough to hear it, I knew beyond any question my mother believed it absolutely. As I approached the difficult years of adolescence, when puberty heightened my emotions and my insecurities grew, my mother became very bitter whenever I went to a friend's house or had a sleepover there. She made little attempt to conceal her jealousy and I was forced to find ways of avoiding or, if that was not possible, of putting up with her outbursts.

Until the summer of 1996 this was just faint background noise in an otherwise happy family landscape; something I had to be aware of, a little speed bump to be navigated, but nothing which really threatened to unravel the fabric of our lives. And if it ever got to be a problem, I could always count on my father being there to make everything right again. Until the day he wasn't.

One Saturday morning I woke up early. It wasn't a school or work day and I presumed my parents would still be asleep in their bedroom on the floor below mine. Normally, I would have stayed in bed, relishing the prospect of a lazy weekend lie-in, but that morning something made me get up and go downstairs.

I found my father sitting quietly on the couch in the living room; he didn't immediately say anything, and I noticed that the front door was unlocked – unusual for this time on a weekend morning. When I asked why, he said my mother had gone to my grandfather's house. This, too, was out of the ordinary; although she visited her father often, it was rare for her to go without either taking me along or at least telling me in advance that she wouldn't be home when I woke up.

And then my father told me – quietly and, as far as I can recall, without any obvious emotion – that he was leaving. He didn't attempt to break this to me gently, didn't try to soften the blow, nor can I remember him holding me or speaking any words of comfort. I was simply presented with a decision he had made to abandon us; that the break-up of our safe little family was a *fait accompli,* and that nothing I could say would change his mind.

In all honesty, at that moment I wasn't capable of saying anything. I was in complete shock and although I didn't want him to leave, I don't think I told him so. I certainly didn't burst into tears or beg him to stay, although I did later on; I think I just sat on the couch with him, numb and confused.

It's hard to recall exactly how I reacted because from then on, I began having strange lapses of memory; whenever I experienced shocks, my mind seemed to shut down and resist any subsequent attempts to recall the traumatic events immediately beforehand. With hindsight, I know that this is a protection mechanism, something my subconscious does independently to protect me from otherwise unbearable events. I don't fully understand how this process works: I only know that it does – and that it began that summer morning when I was eleven years old.

It was – or at least it felt like – just a few minutes after he dropped his bombshell that my father bundled me into the car and drove me to my grandfather's house. I don't believe we spoke on the short journey, and I'm fairly sure he didn't take me inside – he just dropped me at the door and drove off without saying goodbye.

I know that every day millions of children face the misery of their parents splitting up. It is always traumatic and – except in families where the departure of an abusive parent comes as a welcome relief – more often than not, it leaves a psychological scar on the children. But on its own, family break-up does not set a child on an unavoidable path to prostitution; however abruptly and callously I was given the news, I didn't end up selling my body to strangers in the Red Light District just because my parents separated. The picture is – as it always is – rather more complex.

It is the way adults handle their divorce that determines how well (or badly) their children cope with the disintegration of their family. Good parents place their children's welfare first and work hard to limit the fallout from the emotional carnage they have caused. Others, whose break-up is acrimonious and overwhelming, find it difficult to protect their children from the backwash of their own toxic stew of resentment and bitterness. But the worst parents are those who use their children as weapons; turning already traumatised youngsters into proxy soldiers in adult wars is a guaranteed recipe for trouble. My mother fell squarely into this last category.

As my father drove away, I went into my grandfather's house to look for my mother. I found her in an upstairs bedroom; I wanted her to put her arms around me, to hold me and comfort me and tell me everything would be alright. I needed what any child in those circumstances would need: love and security. My mother offered neither.

Her very first words were a blunt and unreasonable question: who, she demanded, did I want to live with? Of course, I didn't know; it was less than an hour since my father had told me he was leaving and even if I had been old enough to think about it rationally, I'd had no time to think about what this meant in practical terms. And yet my mother stood there expecting me to take sides, confronting me with a choice that no child should be forced to make. I couldn't give her a sensible answer; instead I blurted out the first thing that came into my head, saying that I didn't really know, but perhaps I should live with my father.

Unsurprisingly, this wasn't what she wanted me to say. She looked at me coldly and said, 'If you go to live with him, I shall hang myself.' It was a terrible thing to say to a child, especially one in shock; it placed all the responsibility for her welfare – her survival – on me. I don't know whether I truly believed she would commit suicide, but I understood instinctively that if she did, it would be my fault. And so I promised there and then that I wouldn't leave her, that I would stay with her, comfort her, assuage her pain. In doing so, in making that enforced and impossible choice, I set the pattern for our lives over the coming years. I couldn't have realised it then, but by suppressing my childish needs and prioritising her adult ones, I was giving her permission to transfer the weight of her unreconciled emotions and unhappiness on to my eleven-year-old shoulders.

That morning marked two indelible changes in my young life. It was the moment my childhood ended and I was forced to carry the burdens of an adult. And it was the moment I began to hate my mother.

Over the next few days she told me why my father had left us. It was the usual banal story behind break-ups the world over: he had been having an affair. He had always been flirtatious around other women, but he had fallen in love with one of them. Whether or not she had known or suspected this for some time, his decision to move in with his new girlfriend left my mother feeling predictably discarded and unloved. Unfortunately for us, she found this rejection utterly unbearable and I was drafted in as a weapon to be deployed in her war with him.

Although she had effectively blackmailed me into staying with her, she repeatedly told me that the reason I could not live with my father was that he didn't want me; that he was too busy with his mistress to have any time for me. Ironically, although my mother had no means of knowing this, and made the claims simply to reinforce her adopted role as the victim and martyr in our family's commonplace tragedy, she turned out to be at least partially correct in her assessment. In the ensuing weeks and months, I spent every other weekend with my father and his girlfriend and whilst he was – on the surface at least – kind and generous, I never again felt that I had his full attention, let alone love.

Nor did the visits help my mother or her increasingly fragile emotional state. Always jealous and needy, she reacted by becoming ever more demanding of me, insisting that I become a replacement for her departed husband. Very soon after my father left, she announced that she could not bear to sleep alone; from then on, I was required to share her bed every night. This took a severe psychological toll; it felt completely wrong to be forced to replace my father in their marital bed, and whilst my mother never sexually abused me – I don't recall her ever actually touching me at this point in our lives – I was once woken in the middle of the night by the sounds and movement of her masturbating next to me.

When the pain of his loss became overwhelming, I was expected to comfort her; no matter that I, too, felt abandoned and was struggling to navigate the choppy waters of my parents' mutual antagonism whilst simultaneously coping with puberty. My mother passed to me all the responsibility for managing her distress.

As the weeks and months wore on, I missed my father more and more – and became increasingly angry with my mother. I cried frequently and began phoning my father in tears, begging him to come back, pleading with him not to leave me alone. It was a wasted effort: he had chosen a new life with his girlfriend. He was happy and wasn't about to abandon that just because I (let alone my mother) needed him.

Perhaps if I had been able to talk to my mother about this, we could have found a way through the pain. But it was impossible; she was too wrapped up in her own grief to take care of me. She constantly denounced my father for leaving us and I soon learned to keep my phone calls to him a secret; I knew that if she found out she would be angry and take out all her pent-up rage on me.

And so, unfairly in many ways, I came to blame my mother for the break-up of our once happy family. We fought frequently and soon I began running away – not for long, and I never went very far – in the hope that she would notice my distress and put aside her own needs to look after me. But she never did. Instead, we more or less moved into my grandfather's house and my mother turned over much of the responsibility for my care to her father and her brothers. They proved as insensitive as she had been. Faced with a moody, depressed and now troublesome adolescent, they invariably took my mother's side in any argument. 'Your mother is in a lot of pain because your father left her,' they told me. 'You need to behave better for her sake.'

I wanted to scream, I wanted to shout, to make them recognise that my mother wasn't the only one suffering – that I, too, was hurting badly and that I, too, missed my father terribly. Above all, I think I wanted them to see that it was unfair to expect a child to carry the whole burden of her mother's mental anguish. But I didn't – couldn't – tell them. Always shy and insecure, I drew further back inside my shell; I became increasingly isolated, hiding my emotions and erecting mental barricades against the world. I was not yet twelve years old and I felt dead inside.

What I really needed – other than the love and attention of a functioning parent – was someone to talk to. There's an old saying – 'misery loves company', and that's certainly part of it, but really it was much more fundamental than that. If I was to find any way out of the psychological prison walls I was building around me, I desperately needed to find a friend; someone who instinctively understood what I was going through because they, too, were struggling.

Which is how I met Olivia.

TWO

Olivia: A Child in the Middle

I longed for my parents to separate. Always. All of my life. I can't remember a time when I didn't go to bed at night, hoping and praying that I when I woke up, I would find that they were getting divorced. I knew that was the only way the fighting would stop.

I was born – nine days after Anna – in one of Amsterdam's sprawling southern suburbs. I was the second child in our family; my sister, Eva, had been born two years earlier, but unlike her, I was a sickly infant. Three months after I was born, I developed chronic eczema and asthma, and the damage to my lungs was so serious that throughout my early childhood I was regularly taken to the local hospital and kept – sometimes for weeks at a time – in an isolation ward.

All of our extended family lived near us. We spent most time with my maternal grandma; she had been widowed before I was born, so she had the time and – as I would come to discover – the much-needed patience to help my mum with the daily demands of family life. We did not have the same relationship with my dad's side of the family. For reasons which were never explained, my mum disliked Dad's parents and brothers and we only saw them on the rare occasions when she could be persuaded that a visit was unavoidable.

Our neighbourhood was not a great place to grow up; it was a little run-down and beginning to suffer from the drugs and crime that were slowly creeping out from the city centre into the suburbs. When I was four, my parents decided that we needed to move somewhere quieter and less troubled, and they bought a large house with a big garden on the corner plot of a newly built terrace in the same village as Anna's family, around thirty kilometres from where we used to live. There was a lovely park right next door and it was safe, so my sister and I could run out to play on the swings and the roundabout unsupervised.

To our neighbours, and to friends, we must have seemed like a perfect middle-class family. Both my parents had good jobs – my dad had a senior position in a Dutch government agency and my mother worked as a book-keeper in the office of an agency for people with Down's Syndrome – we had a lovely home and money was never a problem. We went on holiday every year, either skiing in Austria or soaking up the sun in Spain or Greece. I enjoyed all the typical privileges of a comfortable childhood: swimming lessons, gymnastic classes and my particular favourite, the Girl Scouts. I looked forward to the annual summer camp, where for a whole week we ran free in the local woods, our uniforms emblazoned with the organisation's motto: 'To Save and to Serve'. All of us learned and took to heart the Dutch Scouts' laws: help out at home, obey without complaining, care for our health and never, ever, look down on anyone because of the job they do.

That, then, was how the Smit family would have seemed to anyone on the outside. But I knew different; I experienced it from the inside – and behind our closed front door it was a battleground in which my sister and I were caught in the middle of our parents' bitter and unending war.

My mum was bipolar. Her moods swung violently between bursts of manic activity and debilitating hopelessness, and her condition was made worse by post-natal depression. She was never able to fully bond with my sister and me, nor look after us properly; she took to her bed for days on end, leaving us crying in wet and dirty nappies. I know now that she couldn't help this, that she was a prisoner of these twin conditions, but as we grew from infancy to early childhood, we felt that she simply didn't love us as a mother should. The best she could manage – and even then, not consistently – were the basic necessities of childcare: feeding us and making sure we were dressed.

My dad struggled to cope with my mum's volatility. He was always under great stress at work and when he came home, she essentially drained him of what little strength he had left. They argued constantly – especially if Dad had to work late or if he came back from the office later than she expected, and as often as not, the smallest, most trivial things would set her off. Visits to his relatives were almost guaranteed to result in a row; my mum hated his side of the family and invariably attacked him over some petty slight she believed my grandfather, uncles or aunts had inflicted on her.

Her drinking made things worse. Although she had been warned that alcohol would interfere with the medication she took to control her illness, she turned to the bottle for comfort; the result was like throwing petrol on a smouldering fire.

My dad was simply unable – or unwilling – to handle my mother's mood swings and sharp tongue. His response was swift, brutal and unforgiving – and he used his fists to deliver his message. Their fights invariably began with simmering anger and insults, escalated to vicious screaming matches and then progressed to an inevitable conclusion in which he picked up the nearest object – plates and glasses were his favourite weapons – and hurled them across the room at her. When this didn't work, he grabbed her, pushed her over and started hitting her.

However much my mum infuriated him, Dad's behaviour was unforgivable. Worse, neither of them made any attempt to hide these violent outbursts from their children. The fights usually started as we all gathered to eat supper; night after night, my sister and I would sit at the table while our parents hurled insults at each other over the evening meal. But often – too often – I found myself quite literally in between them as they fought. My sister tried to hide on the other side of the room but I always wanted to protect my mum and I deliberately pushed myself in front of her as Dad screamed in her face, me begging him to stop. It never made any difference. On one occasion – I can't have been much more than five years old – I got between them while he was hitting her and tried to push him away. In the heat of his fury, I don't think he even noticed; he just ignored me and carried on trying to beat her as she lay on the floor.

These fights lasted for hours. Once they had started, nothing seemed to give my parents pause for thought. My sister and I frequently put ourselves to bed to the sound of their arguments and although – I still don't know how – we eventually fell asleep, we would be woken later by thumps and the smashing of crockery or the sound of Mum's crying. We got up, crouched at the top of the stairs and watched, waiting for the storm to blow itself out.

The strangest aspect to these bouts of violence was that after they were over, no one ever talked about what had happened. My parents never made any attempt to reassure their two frightened children; instead, however late the hour, my mother usually scooped us up, bundled us into the car and drove us over to stay at my grandmother's house. And I was relieved when she did; although it was unsettling to leave home, and the sleeping arrangements – a shared mattress on the floor in the living room – were uncomfortable, I was just happy to be away from the arguments and out of range of my dad's fists.

These respites never lasted long. Each time we turned up on my grandmother's doorstep I hoped that we would stay for ever, but each time Mum took us back home after a few days. Life then resumed as if nothing had happened: once we were back inside our own front door, my parents never once mentioned the fight, or us leaving. And despite the beatings my dad dished out, my mum never reported him to the police; I don't think it would ever have occurred to her to do so.

Growing up in that house felt like sitting on a powder keg, and the uncertainty of not knowing when my parents' next fight would erupt inevitably had an effect; my sister and I began running away to find a few hours' peace, hoping against hope that we might come home to a warm, loving embrace from adults who had worried themselves sick at our disappearance. When that didn't work – and it rarely did – Eva's way of coping was to shrink into the background, but I wasn't built that way; the more the cycle of violence, separation and uneasy truce repeated itself, the more confrontational, the more angry, I became. I started to hate my dad and resent my mum.

Looking back, I realise that she couldn't help her illness and at least some of the behaviour it drove her to. But I also think that she realised the power this gave her and used it as a way of drawing sympathy and attention to herself. Although she never talked to me after I had witnessed one of their arguments, she did subtly try to recruit me to her side in the war of attrition that constituted her marriage. Mum told me often – so often that it became an immutable part of my childhood understanding – that when I was eight months old, my dad had hit her as I sat on her lap. I was far too young to have had my own memory of this incident, but her constant repetition of the story fed the nascent contempt I felt for him.

Mum also tried to drive a wedge between me and Dad by never disciplining me herself. However difficult my behaviour became – and as the years went on, I was definitely difficult – she never raised her hand to me. Instead, she would send me to my room and tell me to wait for my dad to get home. I would look out of my window, watching to see him pull into the drive – at which point I hid under the bed. He came upstairs, dragged me out, pulled down my pants and spanked me. I can't say he ever went beyond normal discipline – or at least, normal for that time in our village where it was not uncommon for dads to smack their children – but with hindsight, I realise that by making him the one to dish out punishment, my mum was deliberately manipulating me, co-opting me as a foot soldier in her never-ending battles with him.

Why did they stay together? I really don't know. I wanted them to divorce; I prayed and prayed that they would. Mum often promised that she would find a new house, that she would take me and my sister away, to live somewhere safe, free from Dad's anger and away from the broken crockery and bruises that invariably accompanied it. But she never did; to this day they are together, still in the same house, still fighting, still miserably unhappy.

I'm as sure as I can be that people outside our family realised what was happening; my grandmother definitely knew and I think our neighbours must have heard the sounds of the fights through the walls and seen the bruises. But no-one intervened. I think that a lot of people don't know what to do in that situation and, in any case, to outsiders my father must have seemed like a good, normal family man.

Nor did my teachers do anything. They, too, must have realised that something was wrong, since I was a difficult and argumentative student who had very few friends. Unfortunately, my parents had chosen to send me to a Montessori school, which didn't impose structure or discipline on its pupils; instead, it let us choose for ourselves whether or not to go to lessons. I rarely bothered, spending most of my time making and serving coffee to the staff, and none of them ever asked why I refused to attend classes.

Eventually, though, my parents realised this was a problem. The first years of a child's education are amongst the most vital for their development, and I was falling dangerously behind my classmates. And so, shortly after my ninth birthday, they withdrew me from the Montessori school and sent me instead to the local primary school in our village; it turned out to be just what I needed. I responded immediately to the structure and discipline the teachers imposed, and for the first time I began to succeed academically; I even found myself enjoying lessons.

Perhaps if Mum and Dad had been able to provide the same atmosphere at home, my life would have turned out differently. But they were too wrapped up in their own vicious warfare to see that their children desperately needed safety and security, not exposure to endless arguments and violence.

Deception and lies were the lessons Mum taught us at home, and I learned early on to keep secrets; I understood that I was not allowed to confide in anyone about my parents' constant arguments, Mum's mental illness or the violence Dad inflicted on her. Ironically, though, my mum didn't feel these rules applied to her; whilst she never (as far as I knew) spoke to her family, friends or work colleagues about the beatings, she happily passed on everything that I or my sister told her in confidence.

When puberty arrived, I had become too isolated to discuss the alarming onset of my first period with either of them; worse, I felt too ashamed to ask for their help. I was eleven when I saw the first tell-tale signs of blood in my underwear and my immediate thought was that I could not – I must not – allow my mum to find out. I pulled off my panties, sneaked out of the house and ducked down a nearby alley; here, my face burning with humiliation, I threw the soiled garment down a storm drain.

From then on, I became increasingly troubled; I was rebellious, argumentative and confrontational. I fought with anyone who tried to tell me what I should do, and when conflict erupted – whether at school or at home – I refused to take a backwards step. With hindsight, I realise that I must have come across as a difficult, wayward child, but there was a reason I behaved as I did. I was reacting to the never-ending conflict between my parents and a deep well of anger was building up inside me; I just didn't know what to do with it other than to challenge everything and everybody.

I was eleven when I became friends with Anna. Although we lived five minutes apart and had been at the same village school for more than a year, we hadn't really spoken. Both of us were somewhat solitary and not part of the group of kids who hung out together in the playground or after class.

But somehow, in our final year of elementary education, our paths crossed; we bonded immediately and were very quickly inseparable. From the outside we must have looked like complete opposites: physically I was tall, dark-haired, loud and aggressive, whilst Anna was slight, blonde and quietly shrank away from any conflict. But together we formed one formidable whole child; my *ying* added to Anna's *yang* rendered us – at least in our adolescent minds – impervious to the dangers of the adult world around us. Above all, we recognised in each other something deep and unspoken: that we both missed the love, structure and emotional safety of a functioning family.

And so we became that for each other. Never again would we feel isolated; never again would we be alone. From that moment on, we would love and look after each other; where I went Anna would go, and what Anna did I would do.

We had no idea – how could we have known? – just how dangerous this would turn out to be.

THREE

Anna: Delinquent

I was twelve years old when my mother slapped me hard in the face. It was the first time she had ever hit me, and it hurt all the more because I had brought her a present of a single red rose.

If my mother's brief outburst of violence was unexpected, it was not entirely unjustified: she had just discovered that I had been playing truant for the past fortnight – and that I had forged her signature on a letter explaining my absence to the school.

It was 1997. Olivia and I were in our first year at high school, and soon to take our first tentative steps down the road that would lead to the Red Light District. Ironically, given what was to follow, it had been my mother who initially helped bring us together. The day we really bonded, I had been disciplined at home for some minor offence and not allowed out to play with my usual friends. But because Olivia was new, someone my mother didn't really know and, most importantly, not one of my classmates whose presence in my life she resented, I was allowed to leave the house to play with her.

We always had so much fun, playing and talking to each other at school, finding in each other both a kindred troubled spirit and a respite from our unhappiness, that from that day forward we were never separated. We became – quite literally, as things turned out – as thick as thieves.

I don't think there was a specific incident that caused us to skip school for the first time. It was just that everything in our home lives was falling apart so badly that lessons – sitting in class studying maths, history or geography – didn't seem terribly useful or relevant. We both independently reached the point where simply staying away felt like a perfectly logical thing to do.

It was Olivia who came up with the idea to write notes to the school, faking our parents' signatures and saying that we were too ill to come to class. Although I was more than ready and very willing to play truant, she was the one with the guts to actually say out loud that we should do it. As usual, I was too timid, too afraid of being caught, to initiate the plan; I needed Olivia to take the lead and make it happen.

And so every morning we rode off on our bikes in the direction of school and then when we were out of sight, we turned off the road and cycled towards the other side of the village. We knew, of course, that we couldn't go back to our homes since our mothers were quite likely to be there; in any event, I wasn't allowed to have a key to my house – another of my mother's arbitrary rules. So for two weeks we spent seven hours a day just hanging around on the streets or in the shopping mall, doing nothing, killing the hours until, at the time we would be expected to finish school, we pedalled back to our respective homes.

It couldn't last. We were far too immature to foresee the consequences of our actions, but it was inevitable that sooner or later our continuing absence from class would be questioned. After two weeks the teachers phoned our mothers to ask if we were still sick – and the immediately the game was up.

Somehow we must have got wind that our scheme had been busted. Both of us knew we had to go home and face our mothers' anger, and so we each bought a single red rose to hand over as a peace offering. Looking back, it was a remarkably childish gesture, but then that's exactly what we were – children. And, of course, it didn't work. After my mother slapped my face, she shouted at me and grounded me for a week; Olivia's transgression led to yet another prolonged family argument.

In many ways, our parents' reactions were not uncommon or unreasonable, at least for the time. Our actions were hardly original; children the world over skip school and, when caught, are then punished in very similar ways. And so, while I could handle the physical punishment I received, it was their complete lack of interest in asking *why* we had done it that really hurt. After all, until then we had both been decent students and had always brought home reports showing good grades for our studies. But they didn't; they were too caught up in their own lives and unhappiness to notice that something was going wrong with their daughters.

Subliminally we both understood that, at the age of twelve, we were now on our own. It seemed pretty clear that by punishing our behaviour without trying to find out what had caused it, our parents weren't concerned about what was making us unhappy; they were simply annoyed that that we had caused them additional problems.

And the incident taught us another important lesson. From that day forward we learned to be much smarter in the way we broke the rules; we didn't stop skipping school, but we became more cunning in finding ways not to get caught. Mostly this involved turning up and registering at the start of the day, then slipping out of the gates when the teachers' backs were turned, and spending the next few hours roaming the streets on our bicycles. Soon enough this led us into more trouble.

By then both of us smoked. We had grown up in households where all the adults puffed away on cigarettes and so it was perfectly natural for us to do the same. Unlike our parents, however, we weren't just using tobacco.

Holland has long been famous – or infamous, depending on your point of view – for its tolerant attitude to drugs. Years before we were born, the government effectively decriminalised cannabis, and 'coffeeshops' (cafés that openly and legally sell small amounts of marijuana or hashish) opened across the country. Our little village had one of them.

In theory, you had to be eighteen to buy it, but this law was never enforced. Everyone at our school smoked weed; it wasn't seen as a big deal and although some parents worried about it, others saw it as just a normal part of life. We had our first joints around the time we began playing truant. At first it made me violently sick and Olivia teased me about puking up on the pavement. But that soon passed and I found the sweet smoke eased the anger and unhappiness swirling around in my mind; blotting out the pain with weed quickly became part of our routine.

Typically, we would set off from home and skin up (roll a joint) as soon as we were out of sight; then, after signing ourselves into school, we bunked off for another day of mooching around the streets or the shops. We found it remarkably easy to get our daily supply of drugs; although we were only twelve, and not allowed to go into the coffeeshop to pay for it for ourselves, we simply hung around outside, asking adult customers to buy us enough for a few joints. Rarely, if ever, did anyone question why two schoolchildren were handing them money for drugs; I don't recall anyone ever refusing to do so.

Our parents knew we were using weed. Cannabis smoke has a particular smell that clings to clothes and hair. We had no way of washing it off, so we must have reeked of weed when we got home. Our eyes, too, were red and small, and we constantly had 'the munchies' – the overpowering desire to eat sweets or crisps, which is one of the most basic telltale signs of someone smoking a lot of dope. Sometimes my mother remonstrated with me, telling me she wanted me to stop; occasionally she grounded me when I plainly hadn't. My father was, by then, living with his girlfriend in Amsterdam and didn't seem bothered one way or the other. Olivia's parents were equally disinterested.

Nor did they – or anyone else – ask where we got the money to buy them. Our weekly pocket money would have barely covered the price or one or two joints, yet we were smoking several times a day. We had to be getting the cash from somewhere else. And we were.

Not long after we began playing truant, I stole for the first time. It was during one of our regular afternoons hanging around on the streets and we were out of tobacco. We strolled into a convenience store and I surreptitiously lifted a pack of cigarettes; the owner didn't see me and we escaped outside to light up. Of course, I realised what I'd done was dishonest; our families might have been dysfunctional but both of us had been brought up to know the difference between right and wrong, and straight away I felt ashamed. And yet at the same time there was something exciting about it; I felt as if we were challenging the adult world which – to our juvenile minds – was letting us down so badly. And so we carried on shoplifting. More packets of cigarettes, bars of chocolate, bags of sweets. Once we even stole a kitten from a pet shop, which we gave to friends of Olivia's sister. The only slight saving grace of this otherwise utterly irresponsible theft was that they loved that cat and gave it a good home for many years afterwards.

It was Olivia who came up with the idea of shoplifting to fund our growing dependence on weed. During our days skipping school we had met a group of older teenagers who had made the street corners their home; none had a job or any discernible legitimate income, which made us suspect they had other, less legal ways of earning money. And that is how we progressed from small-scale shoplifting of cigarettes and confectionery into regular raids on clothes shops in the shopping mall.

We became adept at taking garments from the racks and stuffing them undetected into our bags. We kept very little of this haul – just a few bits of clothing which took our fancy. We sold the vast majority, for cash, to our new friends on the streets, and spent the proceeds on the cannabis we needed to make ourselves feel better. A mature adult might have seen that this was a self-defeating circle – that we were stealing to buy drugs to ease the guilt of shoplifting and deaden the unhappiness that had led us to steal in the first place. But we were not adults, we were children, increasingly adrift in a dangerous world. Inevitably, we got caught.

We were thirteen years old when we first saw the inside of a police cell. As was becoming a common occurrence, we'd skipped school and gone to the mall in search of things to steal. A security guard must have been watching us because we were stopped very quickly; I had crammed a few garments in my bag but Olivia hadn't picked up anything. The store detained us until the police arrived, at which point we were taken down to the local station and locked up.

We were held there for several hours until, eventually, my mother arrived. Although I had been caught red-handed with the stolen clothes, there was no real evidence against Olivia. My mother, however, wasn't about to let her get away scot-free; she pointed at Olivia and said: 'She's a shoplifter too. She is always stealing stuff. And it was her who got my daughter involved in the first place.' The officers duly recorded this information in their case files.

Perhaps because we were so young and this was, as far as the police were concerned, our first offence, neither of us was charged. Instead we were given a very strict lecture and a warning that we would not be so lucky next time. When we got home, my mother was – quite rightly – livid. But very quickly her mood changed from anger to self-pity; she told me over and over how sad she was because my father had left us, and stressed that the shame of having to bail her thieving daughter out from a police cell was an additional burden she simply couldn't cope with.

With hindsight, I don't blame her for being angry with me; any parent would have reacted – at least initially – in exactly the same way. But at the time, all I saw was an adult woman who turned the whole wretched situation into an excuse to remind me of her pain and her needs. I was too isolated, too insecure to speak up for myself, but I longed for her to ask me why I was playing truant and shoplifting. I wanted her to realise that I was hurting too; that I missed my father terribly and that I was only getting into trouble as a way of gaining some attention. She never asked. Not once. She made it clear that she was the one who was hurting, and that I had to behave for the sake of her health and her sanity.

As I write this, I realise that it must sound as if I'm trying to excuse my bad behaviour. Honestly, I'm not. I know that I was causing very real problems for my family and that they must have been close to despair about what to do with me. I just wish that someone had thought to wonder why a previously bright, studious, happy child had turned into a weed-smoking juvenile delinquent.

Once she had calmed down, my mother's response to the situation was to ground me for a week and, since she blamed Olivia for everything, she was determined to put an end to our friendship. She went to the school and demanded that the teachers move us into separate lessons, then banned Olivia from coming to see me after class; she even forbade any phone calls between us.

Olivia was always tougher than me and always ready to challenge rules she didn't agree with, so she wasn't about to accept my mother's ban without a fight. As usual, her parents had yelled at her about skipping school and stealing, but they hadn't grounded her. And so, every afternoon, as I was shut up in my room, she cycled up to the front door and pushed a note through the letterbox. They never reached me – my mother waited behind the front door and confiscated each letter as it arrived. However, she couldn't hide their existence from me; I knew that Olivia hadn't given in and would be waiting for me when my punishment was over.

And soon enough it was. My mother couldn't keep me locked up inside for ever, and it wasn't long before we were back in our familiar pattern: skiving off school, smoking weed and hanging around in the mall. We also began to venture outside the relative safety of our village, taking the train into Amsterdam and wandering along the canal-side streets for hours. On one of these occasions we got lost and purely by accident ended up in the Red Light District. We certainly hadn't planned to go there – in fact, I don't think we even knew it existed – but it's in the middle of the city, a short walk from the central station.

We found ourselves in a world of narrow, litter-strewn alleys and neon-lit windows where half-naked women posed and pouted at hordes of tourists and passers-by. And those crowds were huge; we had never seen so many people jammed into such a confined space, jostling each other and making vulgar comments about the girls behind the glass.

For the first time in our truanting adventures, we felt scared. As well as the tourists, we also saw groups of tough-looking men, hanging out on the streets or lounging in bars; we didn't realise then that they were pimps, keeping an eye on their merchandise, for the simple reason that we didn't really understand what the women standing in their underwear in the windows were doing there. We didn't realise they were selling their bodies; much less what that involved.

In all honesty, although we felt frightened, we also experienced a shiver of excitement. We had a sense of being somewhere forbidden and dangerous – a grown-up environment that was thrilling as well as scary. We were only twelve and, other than our mothers, we had never seen an adult naked, or even near naked; the women in the windows, in their skimpy lingerie and microscopic bikinis, struck us as somehow glamorous. We simply didn't have the maturity or experience to process what we were seeing.

Yet what was most surprising – at least when I look back – is that no one questioned what we were doing there. It was evening, growing dark and here were two very young girls wandering around the Red Light District. Although there are no laws against minors walking through the district, I was particularly small for my age and Olivia wasn't that much bigger, so it seems strange that no passers-by questioned why we were there by ourselves. No one stopped us. No one said anything. Knowing what we know now, alarm bells should have rung – someone should have been very concerned. But, as we would later learn the hard way, those streets are a law unto themselves (or at least to the men who control them for profit). They are the commercial equivalent of a military 'free-fire' zone; no one asks awkward questions for fear of upsetting a very profitable apple cart.

It wouldn't be long, though, until sex itself came into our own lives. Like most girls, we had casual boyfriends, but we were both still virgins. Then, when we were thirteen, we went out one night with Olivia's sister, Eva, Eva's boyfriend and his brother, and at the end of the evening we all went back to the brother's house. There was only one bed – which Eva claimed for herself and her boyfriend – while Olivia and the other boy, who was several years older than us, shared a mattress on the floor. Sex inevitably ensued and Olivia lost her virginity in circumstances that underlined the increasingly rootless nature of our lives – and our co-dependence. When I asked her about it the next morning she shrugged and said it hadn't been a big deal; she didn't really care for the boy and said that although she had been nervous, the act itself had turned out to been something of an anti-climax.

For once, I wasn't ready to follow her lead; I wanted my first sexual experience to be romantic and memorable. I wanted it to mean something and so it would be almost two years before I was ready to go to bed with a boy.

We spent the intervening years spinning ever further out of control. We carried on skipping classes, smoking weed and hanging around the mall. And of course we shoplifted, usually expensive clothes, to fund our growing use of drugs. We had begun to hang around with groups of older men and women who loitered on the streets of the village; they had no jobs but were never short of money, and were very happy to pay cash for the items we had stolen.

After that first encounter with the police, we were arrested and marched to the police station at least another four times. We were never taken to court; the detectives seemed to hope that our parents would control us. Unfortunately, they were either unable or unwilling to do so; on one occasion, Olivia's father was summoned to pick us up from the cells but when he turned up, he pulled out a big bundle of clothes he had taken from her wardrobe, laid them out on the counter and, one by one, said, 'This one is stolen, so is this . . .'. It seemed very clear to us that he saw it as the police's responsibility to discipline his wayward daughter and eventually they did. We were hauled before a juvenile panel – much less formal than an adult court – and both ordered to do community service. Olivia was initially sent to a farm where she was required to clean out the pigeons' cages, but soon she joined me at an old peoples' home where I was working out my punishment, serving the residents' meals.

To our surprise, we found that we enjoyed doing this; it felt good to be useful and to put something back into the community from which we had been stealing. But when we had finished our sentences, we quickly fell back into the same old ways, hanging out with the same groups, smoking more and more weed to ease the unhappiness which hung over us like a cloud.

By the age of fifteen, I was sleeping at Olivia's house most of the time, and my father would turn up to collect me from there. One night I overheard him talking to Olivia's parents, telling them that I was weak-minded. I could hardly believe my ears. The man I had worshipped throughout my childhood, and who I had longed to live with, stood in my best friend's house, denouncing me to her family; it hurt me more than anything else in the years since he had abandoned us.

It was against this unsettled background that I decided I was ready to lose my virginity. I'd become close with one of the young men in the group we hung out with; he was seventeen and we weren't exactly dating, but we did like each other and although I did not feel especially close to him on a personal level, I did feel ready to lose my virginity, and so we sat down and decided how, where and when we would to go to bed together. It seemed like a huge step to me – the moment I would, at least in my own head, cross the threshold from adolescence into adulthood – and I wanted it to feel genuinely romantic.

Olivia knew how much this meant to me and so she offered to help make it happen. We chose an evening when his parents would be away, and during the afternoon Olivia rode over to his house; together they set candles around the bed, made sure the lighting was low and the bed soft with freshly laundered linen.

We had, unfortunately, failed to factor in my mother. That morning she and I had another of our bitter arguments and, as usual, her response was to ground me. In the evening my would-be lover waited in vain for me to turn up, until eventually Olivia got word to him that I was once again locked up at home.

In all honesty I can't really blame my mother for the collapse of our scheme. She had no idea of the significance of the day, and she was pretty much at the end of her tether with me anyway. But the result of her punishment was that the carefully planned tenderness of my first sexual experience had to be abandoned; when it happened, a few weeks later, it was a hurried coupling in the distinctly unromantic setting of one of his friend's beds. With hindsight, Olivia and I are able to laugh about the incident; but I wonder, too, whether our respective unsatisfactory and furtive entries into the world of sex left an imprint on our teenage subconscious minds – and whether in some way it pointed towards what we were to become.

Shortly after this, my mother finally had enough of my behaviour and kicked me out of the house for good. She phoned to say that she had bundled up all my possessions in a bin sack and stuffed them in the garden shed – a location she had chosen since, of course, I wasn't allowed a key to our home; I was to collect my stuff and then take a train into Amsterdam to live with my father.

For all the problems between us, being thrown out of home was a shock. Olivia came with me to give me support, but when we unlocked the shed door and looked in the sack, I found that the only thing my mother had packed for me were my birth control tablets; there were no clothes, no underwear – nothing but a handful of pill packets. She was – very obviously – sending me a message, and I reacted with predictable anger. I grabbed a pair of garden shears, used them to smash one of the house windows and we clambered inside. We went straight up to my bedroom, but there was no sign of any of my things. It turned out that my mother had thrown all my clothes in a downstairs cupboard; it took us a while but we eventually found her hiding place, stuffed all we could carry in a bag and set off for my father's house in the city.

Living with him was never likely to be easy. In the years since my father had left us, I think he had undergone a mid-life crisis. He had become much more materialistic than I remembered; everything – from clothing to the décor in his house – had to be designer-branded. During my previous weekend stays at his house, he had showered me with expensive clothes, partly, I think, in an attempt to make up for abandoning me, but also because he seemed preoccupied with worrying about outward appearances and what his friends and neighbours thought of him. It was all about status; my appearance reflected on him, and therefore he was determined to ensure that I looked good.

He was also working harder than ever and often stayed late at the office. Not unreasonably, I was expected to earn my keep by cleaning the house and making the evening meal. But he didn't seem to feel the need to let me know if he was going to be in late, and so the food I had cooked was frequently ruined. It became, as small irritants often do in stressful circumstances, a cause of major rows between us. He had always been a dominant figure throughout my childhood, but now that I was very plainly on a dangerous path he became completely overbearing; he lectured me for hours about how badly I was behaving (as indeed I was) and if, through sheer exhaustion, I fell asleep he shook me awake and began all over again. It was a miserable time and I felt utterly wretched; whenever I saw a film, or an advert on TV, which featured a happy, smiling family, I burst into tears because that was the life I dreamed about. I wanted – desperately – parents who loved and cared for me.

One evening, it became too much. As we sat on opposite sides of the living room and my father launched into his latest diatribe, I reminded him of what he had told Olivia's parents about me. 'What do you expect from a daughter like me,' I shouted; 'someone who is so weak-minded?' He jumped up and aimed a vicious kick at my face; thankfully he missed, but he quickly grabbed me and pushed me across the room, slapping me as I reeled backwards. The noise woke his girl-friend, who was asleep in bed; but when she ran downstairs to intervene, my father screamed at her until she fled back to the safety of the bedroom.

It was the first and only time my father hit me, but it broke the last real emotional bond between us. For all the pain it had caused, I had been able to forgive him walking out on my mother but this was one betrayal too far. From that moment on, I would never again think of him as someone I could trust or rely on, and he very quickly gave up any attempt to care for me.

Reading this, I'm conscious that you might be thinking Olivia and I were out of control, that we were a constant nightmare for our schools and our families. And you are right – or at least not altogether wrong. We were certainly hardened and unrepentant truants; we were habitually stoned on cannabis and we did regularly steal and sell the proceeds of our crimes to pay for drugs. But why, in three short years, had we gone from being well-behaved, respectable young girls to weed-smoking delinquents with a criminal record? The answer is love – or the absence of it.

We were not, of course, different from thousands of other young girls of this age. Many children suffer broken home lives; many endure far worse experiences than we did. Olivia and I don't hold our families solely responsible for all that happened to us; we must shoulder some of the blame for our choices. But we were children, and children's minds aren't sufficiently developed to link actions with consequences – that is an adult's job. So, for all that we were undoubtedly contributing to our downfall, so too were the circumstances in which we were growing up.

Nor are we saying that playing truant, shoplifting and smoking weed were the reasons Olivia and I ended up in the Red Light District; plenty of other young girls do some or all of these foolish things and don't end up selling their bodies to strangers. No, these were the *symptoms* of our problems, not the causes; signposts that we were travelling down a perilous path. We were too young to read these signs for ourselves, much less appreciate the danger they pointed to.

We lacked love; we needed – were desperate for – someone to care about us, to give us attention and to help us find our way. We were children at risk; we were easy meat.

FOUR

Olivia: Prey

We never went looking for trouble. We didn't need to. Two teenage girls, out of control, hanging around on the streets, reckless about their safety? Trouble found us, easily and often.

It was early spring, 2000. We gradually fell in with a new and dangerous crowd. Some were, like us, skipping school and shoplifting, but others were considerably older; one of them had her own studio flat in one of the apartment blocks dotted around our village. Mary was nineteen years old and had been at school with my sister and it was through this connection that we met. Although she was Dutch, her family was originally from Thailand, and to my eyes, she was glamorous. My interest wasn't sexual – I have never been attracted to women as lovers. It was rather that she was older, more worldly-wise, and no one seemed to tell her what to do. Above all, she had her own place, and her life seemed exciting; she didn't have a job but she was never short of money. It was an indication of my immaturity that I didn't wonder how she supported herself and paid the rent.

We began hanging out with her during the days when we were playing truant. Sometimes we sat in her flat, telling her about our lives and our shared sense of unhappiness; on other occasions she joined us on our trips to the mall and helped us steal clothes. Before long, we were spending as many evenings as we could with our new friend and confidante. When Anna was grounded – a frequent occurrence – I became even closer to Mary, often sleeping on her couch.

The evenings, though, had a very different feel from the days. Most nights, a large group of people turned up at her apartment; they were much older – in their mid- to late twenties – and most were men. I didn't like the way the atmosphere changed when these guys arrived. From the moment they walked through the door, there was a slight sense of menace; of the safe space we had found with Mary being subtly undermined. She, too, acted differently around them; it was no longer her and us – everything became about these older men and their interests. Those interests turned out to be drink, drugs and sex.

Very few of the men had jobs, but all were flush with cash to spend in bars and clubs. Very quickly we found out where their money came from: cocaine. Neither Anna nor I had ever tried coke or been around people who used it; it must sound ridiculous, but at the age of fifteen, I don't think I ever actually knew anything about it. Now, it was there in front of us; Mary's friends dealt narcotics openly, across the suburban and rural areas outside Amsterdam.

I'd like to say that we were shocked, that seeing the little bags of white powder made us stop and think about what we were getting into. I'd like to tell you that – but I can't. Neither of us questioned the risks of being around drug dealers – much less the morality of their trade in coke. It was, I think now, another sign that we were much, much too young to be in that world; we simply didn't have the intellectual maturity or emotional development to realise the danger. We were stupid – very stupid; but we were really still children, and children do foolish things.

Soon, we started to use harder drugs than the weed we habitually smoked. It was our Queen's Day national holiday when I first tried ecstasy. *Koningsdag* is a massive day of public celebrations throughout Holland; every town and village organises parades, concerts and parties, and many of the millions of people taking part in the festivities dye their hair orange in honour of the Dutch Royal Family's colours. My contribution to the revelries was to drop a little tab of E in the company of Mary and my sister. I told myself that it was an experiment – that I just wanted to see what all the fuss was about – but I found that it made me feel good. For once, my depression lifted and the clouds of misery, which constantly seemed to surround my family and my home life, floated away.

As usual, Anna followed my lead. The next time we were together at Mary's house we both swallowed an ecstasy pill, and I watched her closely, waiting to see the rush of happy feelings wash over her. They didn't – at least not straight away. Instead, she slumped over on the couch and fell into a deep sleep. Eventually the group of older guys arrived and suggested we all go to eat at a nearby kebab shop. We woke Anna up, dragged her out of the flat, and just as we walked into the restaurant, the ecstasy truly kicked in. She had to hold on to someone's arm to keep from falling, but like me, she found that the drug covered her unhappiness in a warm blanket of numbness. We never graduated to anything else – neither of us has ever touched cocaine – but from then on, we relied on E as well as cannabis to blot out our pain and get us through the days and nights.

Soon, though, the pleasurable dream state the drugs induced turned into a waking nightmare. I began to have really bad trips during which I suffered vivid and terrifying hallucinations; I babbled, sobbed, cried, and was completely unable to speak coherently. It should have been a warning. Unfortunately, it wasn't.

I was high on E the first time I slept with the man who was to dominate our lives for the next six years. Ricardo was twenty-six and one of the group of older guys who came to Mary's apartment. He was tall, had a naturally athletic body and a completely shaven head; he had been born in Suriname, one of Holland's former colonies in South America, and had distinctive, dark, coffee-coloured skin.

I can't say I found him physically attractive but he was somehow strangely impressive. He wasn't a big talker, but when he did speak, his voice was deep and resonant, and his occasional contributions to the conversations in the flat seemed serious and considered. On the rare occasions that he smiled, his face appeared friendly, yet at the same time there was a tangible air of danger surrounding him. And so, although I didn't fancy him, I found him exciting.

Unlike many of the other guys, he had a job. It wasn't what you could call a career – he was working in a factory that made window blinds – but he was also dealing cocaine, and as a result seemed to have plenty of money to spend.

There were two other crucial differences between Ricardo and the rest of the group; not only did he have a full-time girlfriend with whom he shared an apartment, but he was also about to become a father. I knew both of these things, but I'm ashamed to say that I didn't give them any thought. Worse, the first time we had sex, we did it in his girlfriend's flat on the very night she was in hospital, giving birth to their child.

I look back and am appalled by the sheer selfishness and irresponsibility of my actions. It's no excuse to say that I was off my face on ecstasy and can't remember how I ended up in bed with Ricardo; all I can tell you is that I did, that it was perfectly voluntary and that while we had sex, Anna was in the next room with one of his friends. As I say, irresponsible and downright stupid.

He was also much more experienced than me and – then, at least – the sex was pleasurable. But at the same time, at the back of my drug-clouded mind, there were the first faint sounds of alarm bells ringing – I knew something was very far from right.

For a start, it was illegal – the age of consent in Holland is sixteen and I was a year away from that. Whilst many girls of fifteen have sex, they do so with someone at least close to their own age, and both are essentially testing out the shallow reaches of adult waters. Ricardo was eleven years older than me, and he most certainly wasn't experimenting – at least not in that slightly innocent teenage way.

Instead – and, again, this is with the benefit of hindsight – I can see that having sex with me was part of a deliberate and cynical plan. He used his sexual expertise to impress and then to quickly overwhelm me.

Three nights after that first sexual encounter, I was at home in my bedroom. Surprising though this may seem, at the time I was actually trying to work hard at school; it was 9.30 p.m and I was just getting into bed, thinking that an early night would help me get up early the next day, when my sister burst through the door. Eva was crying hysterically, sobbing and gibbering so hard that at first I couldn't understand what she was saying. And then I heard her clearly: 'Mary is dead, she's dead, she's been murdered.'

I was so shocked that I couldn't move. I stood frozen to the spot as Eva became more and more manic – throwing things around the room, shouting and crying. Eventually I calmed her down enough to ask how it had happened – but when she told me, I burst into uncontrollable tears.

For the previous few weeks, Mary had been dating a boy she'd met in our local nightclub. He was the adopted son of the mayor of a nearby town and had a history of sniffing glue. That evening he and Mary had got into an argument; her neighbours heard them fighting and called the police. When the officers arrived, they discovered that he had beaten her round the head with a metal pipe before strangling her with his bare hands; he had then placed her body on the bed and calmly lain down next to her to wait for the authorities.

Mary's murder turned my world upside-down. In part this was because I blamed myself for letting her down. I had met her boyfriend on a couple of occasions and sensed that he was dangerous. The last time I saw him was a few days before her death; I had gone to her apartment and was planning to sleep there that night, but late in the evening Mary went out, leaving us alone together. I was taking a shower when suddenly I had a bad feeling – the type that you can't really explain but is instinctual, like walking alone down a dark alley late at night. I sensed danger and knew I had to get out of the flat, immediately. In a panic, I threw on my clothes and ran home.

When I heard he had killed Mary, the incident seemed like a premonition, and guilt nagged away at me. I hadn't told Mary about my uneasy feeling, and I questioned whether my silence had contributed to her death. What made it worse was that she had even phoned me the night before she died, saying that things didn't seem right. She sounded in a bad way, and I should have gone over to see her straight away, but I put her off. Now it felt like I had failed her twice.

Mary's brutal, senseless murder was the point at which our lives spiralled completely out of control. Afterwards, we were angry; deeply and uncontrollably mad at the world and with ourselves. We desperately needed to talk about this with someone, but by then the relationships with our families had deteriorated beyond repair; I think they tried to comfort us, but we were too far gone to let them.

It didn't help that around this time, Anna and I were separated, as a result of our dismal record of playing truant finally catching up with us. Anna's parents asked the school to help and she was sent down into a class of children a year younger than her; but my parents called in the welfare department to deal with me, and I was packed off to a residential facility for troublesome students. For the next three months I was only allowed to go home at weekends. Cut off from Anna, I had no one to talk to. Or almost no one.

Ricardo phoned me every evening. We would talk at night, and into the early hours of the morning, and very quickly I came to rely on him for support and advice; unfortunately, I wasn't able to see that he was using the situation to increase his hold over me, nor that the school itself was providing everything I needed to get my life back on track. In its strict discipline, I found the structure and support I had longed for at home. I was assessed by a psychologist who concluded that there was nothing mentally wrong with me; I simply needed more – and better – adult attention.

For the first time I began to focus on my education. I went to classes from eight in the morning till five in the afternoon and, without drugs numbing my mind, found that it was surprisingly easy to concentrate. I had always thought that I was stupid – my parents had always told me that my sister was much smarter than me – but in the secure residential environment, I flourished academically.

The school wanted me to stay on for another three months, to make up for my lost education and to build up my self-esteem. Initially, this appealed to me, but then I made the mistake of talking it over with Ricardo; he was adamantly opposed and told me to leave as soon as I could. When my first three months was up, I got on the train back home – and fell straight back into his clutches. From that day onward, Anna and I never went back to school, and our lives fell completely apart.

Oddly, although we had had smoked weed for almost four years and regularly used ecstasy, neither of us drank alcohol – now that changed. Under Ricardo's tutelage, we started going out – the three of us together, occasionally with a group of his friends – and began drinking heavily. It was Ricardo, flush with his drug money, who bought the drinks and he didn't break us in gently with wine or beer; it was spirits straight away. Very quickly we spent most nights in bars, getting hopelessly drunk on whisky and Red Bull. We both stopped using drugs – the cannabis was making us paranoid and my bad ecstasy trips had worsened dramatically – and instead drowned our inchoate unhappiness in booze.

I'm ashamed to say I carried on sleeping with Ricardo. But now the dynamic had changed – we couldn't do it in his apartment because his girlfriend and their baby were back home, so we went to his friends' apartments or, more usually, had quick, functional sex in parks or in the stairwells of buildings. There was little tenderness and no affection in these encounters; I wasn't in love with him and I'm absolutely certain that he didn't love me. I was hurting badly and very vulnerable; I needed comfort – and used sex to dull my pain.

Soon the sex became increasingly aggressive; shortly after my return from the residential school he told me he was going to fuck me anally and before I could object, he forced himself into me. I had never done this before – never even considered it – and it was horrifically painful. Ricardo didn't care; he just took what he wanted and presumed I wouldn't refuse. And, in truth, I didn't. Although Anna and I talked it over later, and told each other that the situation wasn't right, we did nothing about it. I think we had both become so completely desensitised and isolated that we were powerless to stop our slide into ever-more destructive behaviour. Ricardo saw this – and exploited it.

Anna and I were at my house when my phone rang. It was Ricardo – and he was furiously angry because his girlfriend had just told him she had found out he was having sex with me. I should, perhaps, have realised this was coming; we hadn't been particularly careful to hide our meetings and it was inevitable that they would be discovered. Ricardo's girlfriend had somehow got hold of my phone number – earlier that day she called me and, caught by surprise, I'd admitted everything; not unreasonably, she then confronted Ricardo.

He ordered Anna and I to meet him at one of his friends' apartments. When we arrived he pulled me inside, dragged me by my hair into the bathroom and punched me in the face. It was the first time he had hit me and I gasped with surprise and pain – but worse was to come. Second later, as I lay sobbing on the floor and Anna watched in shock and panic, Ricardo pulled a gun – an automatic – from his jacket and shoved it in my mouth, screaming, 'Why did you tell my girlfriend? I'm going to kill you now.'

I had never seen a gun before; I certainly didn't know he had one. I was terrified, my heart beating frantically – I was absolutely convinced he was about to shoot me. Somehow I got away from him, grabbed Anna and fled from the flat. The next few moments took place in a blur. We truly don't remember how we managed to escape – I was dizzy from the punches and the trauma of what happened has blotted out some of our memory. The next thing we can recall is the two of us sitting on the bed in my house and together trying to make sense of what had just happened.

We were both in complete shock. But the strange thing is that it never once crossed our minds to go to the police. Even though I now knew Ricardo had a gun, and that he had threatened to kill me with it, I never thought to report him. In part this was, I think, learned behaviour. I had watched my dad hit my mum time after time and seen that she never complained; now I was repeating the lesson this had taught me.

But that was not the whole – or even the most immediate – reason. Because, like countless other men who abuse and brutalise women, Ricardo convinced me the violence was my fault; I had provoked the beating, and even the threat to shoot me, because I had told his girlfriend about the sex. And so I blamed myself.

But we decided that I would stop sleeping with Ricardo and that we would both stop seeing him. In my mind, and in Anna's, the violence and the gun meant it was all over. But I was wrong, it wasn't over – it was just the beginning.

After that night we didn't hear from him for a couple of weeks. But then he started phoning me again, apologising for what he had done while still blaming me for getting him into trouble with his girlfriend. He begged with me not to abandon him, insisting that Anna and I were his friends and that he needed us. I realise now that there was something – one crucial word – missing from this plea: love. In all that he said to persuade me to change my mind, her never told me he loved me. Because, of course, he didn't: he saw something else in Anna and me – money, and a lot of it.

Eventually he wore me down and I gave in and agreed to see him again. What's worse, I promised that this time I would keep it secret from his girlfriend. And so we fell back into the same old routine: going out drinking with Ricardo and his friends, staggering around the streets and behaving completely irresponsibly. He and I carried on having sex as if nothing had happened, screwing outside on park benches or in borrowed beds in his friends' apartments. But deep inside I knew that something had happened, and that it had changed things between us irrevocably. If some of the sex with Ricardo was still pleasurable, I found his sexual preferences increasingly difficult because I realise they were a way of him expressing his dominance and control. But above all, Anna and I were beginning to fear him and the next, inevitable, explosion of violence.

It wasn't long in coming. Most typically the trouble began in a bar: we would be sitting drinking when, without any warning, he would suddenly accuse me of paying too much attention to one of his friends. I hadn't, of course; I was already far too scared of offending Ricardo to flirt with someone else.

But the truth didn't matter and the result was always the same: Ricardo pushed me outside and hit me in the face. Five, six, seven slaps, a couple of punches, the knobbly gold rings on his fingers breaking the skin around my eyes, ears and mouth, drawing blood and leaving me gasping for breath.

At other times he kicked me, sending me – quite literally – flying across the street; or, if we were inside somewhere, he repeatedly pushed my face into a sink full of water, threatening to drown me.

Nor was I his only punch bag. As often as not, he grabbed Anna and demanded she tell him what I had been doing behind his back; since I hadn't been doing anything there was nothing she could say (even if she had wanted to), and he laid into her with his fists. When he was done, and in the sanctuary of my bedroom, we covered the cuts and bruises under thick layers of make-up, hiding the visible signs of our shame – for that is how we saw it.

I would like to tell you that we came to hate Ricardo, but, sadly, I can't. Although we lived in terror of what he would do to us, and had enough common sense to realise that our situation wasn't right or normal, this understanding was completely overshadowed by our unhappiness. Even though Anna wasn't the one sleeping with him, she stayed with me and suffered his beatings because she wanted to protect me but also because, by this point, she was simply too scared of Ricardo to contemplate getting away from him. At some level we knew that he didn't really believe I was cheating on him – and nor would he have cared if I had. Rather, he was using violence, and our daily fear of it, to control us. The early subtle stages of our grooming – the long late-night talks, the pretended interest and feigned sympathy – were finished; now it was all about keeping us in line with vicious beatings. But the most insidious aspect of this control was that we never knew when the violence would erupt, and so we lived in constant fear of a punch in the face.

It worked. By the end of that year, and as we approached our sixteenth birthdays, we were completely under Ricardo's thumb – or, more accurately, his fists. Isolated from our families (despite both still living at home), keeping between ourselves the knowledge of what he inflicted on us, he controlled our lives completely, and we felt powerless to refuse him anything. When he called, we went to him; when he demanded sex, I gave it to him; when he insisted on our silence, we became the keepers of his secrets.

Even when he gave me a sexually transmitted disease, I was made to assume all the responsibility. At the time I knew nothing about STDs, but when I woke up one morning with terrible pain in my abdomen, I realised that something very bad had happened. I was sweating and in agony and the cramps were so powerful that I found I couldn't stand upright; and then I noticed the smell – a vile, sour stink coming from my vagina.

I yelled for my mum; she took one look at me, then drove me straight to the hospital. I made her wait outside the consulting room while the doctor did a test. Very quickly the results came back – I had chlamydia. I was utterly ashamed and begged the doctor not to tell my parents, but he insisted that he had no choice; I was fifteen and therefore still legally a child.

Unsurprisingly, my parents were furious. They hadn't known that I was dating, let alone that I was sleeping with, a man eleven years older than me, who already had a girl-friend and a baby. But the only punishment they imposed was to ground me for one night. As I lay in my room, I phoned Ricardo and told him about the diagnosis. I knew that he had given me the infection because he was my only sexual partner, but his reaction was one of apparent surprise. He said, 'I don't know how I got that,' and implied that the whole miserable business was somehow my fault. And so dealing with the chlamydia for both of us became my responsibility; he ordered me to get him a course of antibiotics because – so he claimed – his own doctor wouldn't prescribe them for him.

This was, of course, nonsense. He had as much right to treatment under our health service as I did. But, as always, I just accepted what he told me and, when my parents allowed me out again, I sorted out the drugs for him. A week or so later he started having sex with me again. And life – if that's what you could call it – returned to what passed for normal.

FIVE

Anna: Hooked

Close your eyes. Imagine you are lying down. Now count, slowly and silently: five seconds, ten, thirty, on and on until it's not seconds but minutes passing. Listen to the sound of your heart beating, the blood pumping around your body as you lie as still and quiet as you can.

Now imagine that you are not alone. Imagine that a heavy, sweaty man's body is pressing down on you; feel his breath on your face, his hands gripping your wrists, his thighs spreading your legs apart. And now brace yourself for the moment when he forces himself into you. You do not want to do this; you are scared and the pain of penetration is suddenly sharp and unforgiving as he begins to move inside you.

Push the hurt deep down inside, concentrate on the sound of your breathing, try to block out the shame of your body being violated for a fistful of banknotes. And now imagine one more thing: you are sixteen years old.

Open your eyes now. Relax. You are not that young girl; you are safe. But you know now what it felt like to be me, one night in May 2001. In all that follows, please try to remember. Because I was that sixteen-year-old girl.

It was just before our sixteenth birthdays in April 2001 and the sky was dark when Ricardo phoned, telling us to meet him on a street corner on the other side of the village. We were, as we always were, together in Olivia's room, sitting on the bed, when his call came – as it came most evenings – summoning her to service his sexual demands while I waited nearby. This night, though, was to be different. He wasn't going to take us out drinking; instead he told us he had come up with a plan to make us all a lot of money.

Whenever we met Ricardo, we followed the same ritual. He and Olivia walked together, talking, while I kept a few paces ahead of them. That evening I was mooching along in front, not really listening to what they said, when I heard them arguing. I turned round and saw him launch a vicious kick at Olivia; his boot hit her body with a dull, sickening thump and she dropped, stunned, down onto the pavement. I looked around to see if there was anyone nearby who might come to help, but the street was empty. I knew then that we were in for another beating and that there was no-one to save us.

Bruised and bloodied, Olivia staggered unsteadily back to her feet and I rushed forward to help her. And then Ricardo was standing over us both, his face flushed with anger. 'There's a man. I know him – he's a friend of client of mine, someone I sell coke to. He is going to pay to have sex with you – now; he's waiting now. Let's go.'

I'm not sure that the full meaning of Ricardo's words sank in straight away. I was shocked and speechless and, at first, couldn't make sense of what he was telling us. Why would a man pay to have sex with us? Why would Ricardo agree, when he had always been so violently possessive of Olivia? Who was this man? And then the horrible reality dawned: this was Ricardo's great plan to make our fortunes. My instant reaction was anger: I wasn't going to have sex with someone I didn't know – especially in some sort of sordid commercial transaction – and I'd be dammed if I was going to allow Ricardo to force Olivia to do so either.

It quickly became clear that she had said exactly the same – which was why Ricardo had knocked her down. Now, facing him together, we started to argue. 'No way,' we said, 'no way are we going to let some man fuck us, no matter how much money he's offered you.' Our brief moment of defiance simply served to enrage Ricardo even more. He marched off, almost daring us to walk away – and, of course, that's exactly what we should have done. But we didn't; he had already conditioned us too well to refuse him outright, so we caught up with him and began pleading with him not to make us do this.

It made no difference – at least no good one. He turned on us and made it absolutely clear that if we continued to argue, he would punch and kick us until we gave in. That, however, wasn't the worst of it. As we stumbled along the street, still shocked and now desperately afraid, Ricardo told us his customer was only willing to pay for sex with one of us; the man would choose his victim – and that's exactly how we perceived ourselves – when we got to his apartment.

I was revolted: Olivia and I were going to be forced to put on some sort of sordid beauty parade – and the 'winner's' prize was to be turned into a prostitute. But, very quickly, this disgust was replaced by a sense of guilt; that it was my fault we were in this mess because I had not stepped in when Ricardo beat and mistreated Olivia. And then I felt something so visceral, so overwhelming, that I knew I could not resist it: a determination to protect my friend, whatever the cost.

To those who knew us then – and to anyone looking at us from the outside – Olivia always seemed the stronger, the more dominant half of our indivisible friendship. Whilst both of us wanted to skip school, smoke weed, take ecstasy, I had usually been too timid to initiate this destructive behaviour; I had needed – and still needed – her recklessness to push me towards the first step, and thereafter relied completely on the reassurance that she was with me and that whatever happened, we were in this together. Now, for the first time, I felt the need to put my body in front of hers and to shield her from the pain and humiliation of being forced to have sex with a stranger for money. I didn't want to be sold to him – of course I didn't – but as we approached the customer's flat, I prayed, silently and fervently, that he would pick me, not Olivia.

By the time we got there, I was shaking and petrified. My stomach went into spasms; vicious cramps tore at my guts and my heart beat so fast and so hard that it seemed in danger of exploding inside my chest. And then Ricardo's customer opened the door.

He was a short, fat ugly Iranian man in his late forties or early fifties. The moment I saw him I thought, 'No – please no.' He was the same age as my father, dirty-looking and his eyes were mean and hard. I stared at his squat, vile body, bile rising in my throat: the idea of having sex with him was too revolting for words. Yet, at the same time, I still hoped he would choose me and spare Olivia.

Ricardo proudly showed off 'his' girls, then asked his customer which of us he wanted. The man walked around us and looked us up and down as if he were inspecting a piece of merchandise; his eyes, greedy with lust, lingered over every inch of our bodies and it felt as if I was already being stripped naked and laid out for his pleasure. And then, almost in slow motion, I saw him raise a cruel, callous finger and wordlessly point at me. My legs shook uncontrollably and my stomach heaved, conscious that inside of me something, some last vestige of pride and self-worth, was dying; yet at the same time I was happy to know that I would be saving Olivia from what was to come.

I watched the Iranian hand Ricardo a wad of bank notes and receive a single, foil-wrapped condom in exchange. The deal was sealed; I had been sold and I knew that there could be no escape. Then, without saying a word to me, Ricardo grabbed Olivia, pushed her out of the door and left me alone with the customer.

The man – I didn't know his name then, and I was never told it – led me into a bedroom. 'Take off your clothes,' he ordered, then, 'Lie down on the bed. Now.' Numbly, I pulled the T-shirt over my head and unbuttoned my jeans, but my hands were shaking so much it felt like it took ages to undo them. I folded them neatly, taking my time so that it in some way delayed the proceedings, before placing them on the floor. My heart was pounding and the sound of my blood pulsing through my veins crashed in my ears. As the man stripped naked, and I saw that his body was even more vile and repulsive than I had feared. I felt nausea rising in my guts.

I was more scared than I had ever been, and couldn't face the extra vulnerability that would come with being completely nude, so I kept my bra and panties on. It didn't seem to bother the man, and he lay down on the bed while I, shivering in my underwear, steeled myself for what he was about to do to me.

Somehow, in my terror, I thought of a way to delay what was to come. Kneeling beside the bed, I began giving his thick, sweaty torso a lacklustre massage. He grunted – apparently in pleasure – and I congratulated myself on buying a little time. But it couldn't last for ever; and he soon issued new instructions. 'Lie back now. Open your legs.' He rolled the condom onto his penis and, pushing my pants to one side, thrust himself inside me. I shut my eyes, determined not to look at him, and tried to find a way of shutting out the pain and humiliation of what was happening to my body.

I don't know how many minutes passed before he groaned and gave one final thrust. In the years since, I have tried to remember the details, but my subconscious has somehow blocked or deleted much of it to prevent my mind from shattering under extreme trauma. What I do recall realising – very clearly – is that I had just been raped.

When he was done, the man rolled off me and went to phone Ricardo, telling him to come and collect me. Slowly and in a daze, I pulled on my jeans and dragged the T-shirt over my head. As my hands brushed my face, I found that I had been crying.

Ricardo turned up with Olivia a few minutes later. All the anger and viciousness that he had displayed on the way to the customer's apartment had vanished. With the man's money safely in his pocket, he was smiling and very evidently happy. Olivia, by contrast, looked miserable and fearful and could barely meet my eyes.

He took us to a bar in the centre of a village and ordered a round of drinks to celebrate what he described as a successful first step on our new business venture. I quickly swallowed the first whisky and ordered another. I looked at Olivia and, without a word being said, knew that both of us needed to get drunk. Alcohol – and lots of it – was the only way we could blot out the evening's events.

It may sound odd, but aside from Ricardo's one comment about our 'partnership', none of us really discussed what had happened. Olivia told me – briefly and without any real emotion – that while I was being raped by the Iranian man, Ricardo had taken her to a nearby park and fucked her. But that was the limit of what was said: no questions were asked, no truths told. At the end of the night Olivia and I were more drunk than we had ever been; we almost fell through the door of her parents' home and collapsed, semi-conscious, on her bed.

To this day, I don't know why we didn't immediately tell our families that Olivia's boyfriend had forcibly prostituted me. Perhaps if we had had stable home lives, we would have been able to sound an alarm. Perhaps if we had felt secure in the warmth of parental love, we could have found the courage to disclose what had happened and to ask for their help in escaping the world we had fallen into. But we didn't; by this point we were now so alienated from our families that it was impossible to confide something so shocking, so shameful to them.

Instead, we clung to each other. And in our fierce, unshakeable love lay the seeds of our future downfall. Why? Because Ricardo recognised it as the key to realising his plans; he saw that we were a 'two for one' deal – and that dominating either one brought both of us under his complete control. By successfully prostituting me, he had hooked the pair of us. From that moment, we were powerless and unable to deny him anything.

Most nights I slept at Olivia's house, but even there we were not safe. Once, when her parents went on holiday, leaving us to fend for ourselves, Ricardo turned up, unannounced. He walked into the kitchen, picked up a large knife then, without explanation, grabbed Olivia's hair, threatening to cut it off, before whacking her repeatedly with the flat of the blade.

It was the arbitrary nature of these attacks that was most debilitating. Ricardo's moods swung so unpredictably – and so fast – between cheerfulness and brutal anger that we lived in a perpetual state of fear. The old phrase 'walking on eggshells' is a cliché, but we lived it, every day. We never knew when or where the next punches would come, only that they were inevitable.

Ultimately we came to see that he was deliberately using the randomness of his violence as a psychological weapon to give him total control over us; he was systematically breaking us down, making sure we were afraid of him. It worked.

And you ask: why? Why did we carry on like this? Why didn't we just say no; walk away or go to the police? It is the question asked of all women who remain in abusive relationships, and part of the answer is in the question itself: violence. We were so hopelessly terrified of Ricardo that we were sure that if we tried to leave, he would kill us – he had, after all, forced a gun into Olivia's mouth and threatened to blow her head off. But beyond that was a deeper problem, and one which explains how manipulative men are able to maintain control over young girls like us, all over the world. Throughout all the beatings we always blamed ourselves: it was our fault he beat us because we had messed up his life with his girlfriend and his child.

At some level we knew this was not right, but we had seen Olivia's father repeatedly hit her mother and knew that, after the briefest of separations, each time she went back to him. So, in some way, staying with Ricardo, trying to placate him and covering our bruises with make-up when that failed, seemed the only course of action open to us. It was learned behaviour. It was all that we knew.

One thing was absolutely guaranteed to provoke Ricardo into giving us a beating. Any suspicion – well founded or not – that we had formed new friendships, or spent time with people he hadn't sanctioned, led, inevitably, to a flurry of punches raining down on our heads. Even though he was still living with his girlfriend – as well as having sex with other women – he believed we were his property, and he was very posses- sive indeed about what he owned. At one point, Olivia got to know a boy in our village. She liked him, partly because he was closer to our own age than Ricardo, but mainly because he was nice to her. One thing led to another one evening; he was a little overenthusiastic when kissing her and left a hickey – a small love bite – on her neck.

Later that night, as we got off the bus near Olivia's house, Ricardo suddenly appeared behind us, seized her and demanded: 'Where have you been? Who have you been seeing?' Olivia quickly tried to hide the tell-tale mark on her throat by turning up her collar. Ricardo snatched at her hand, pulled down the top of her sweater and saw the hickey. He went mad, screaming and demanding to know who had given Olivia the love bite. When she refused to tell him, he grabbed me and hissed at Olivia: 'You're going to talk or I'm going to hit her.' And he did. In the middle of the park, he pummelled my face, the chunky rings on his knuckles leaving deep red marks beneath my eyes. Olivia tried to intervene, begging him to stop and promising that she would tell him everything. He ignored her and kept hitting me, until I agreed to tell him what she had been doing. Again, with the benefit of hindsight, it's obvious that he was manipulating the situation, making Olivia plead for me, and punishing me until I betrayed her. It was a mind game, fucking with our heads just as deliberately as he fucked Olivia and prostituted me to the Iranian. But at the time, all we could think about was how to make the immediate violence stop.

Looking back now, those two years passed in a blur of sex, drink and violence. A couple of weeks after renting me out to his customer, he told us that the Iranian wanted me again. As before, this was an order, not a request, and Ricardo very clearly expected me to comply. And I did; once, sometimes twice, every month for two years I let him take me to his customer's apartment, watched as he exchanged a handful of notes for a condom, and then lay down meekly on the bed while the man fucked me. Each time I tried to send my mind somewhere else, to concentrate on something – anything – except the pain of the sex and the degradation of being prostituted.

I often found myself thinking of my relations. My family's house was no more than one street away and I wondered what my parents, or my uncles, would do if they knew what was happening to me. But these thoughts didn't help; they merely reinforced the shame of what I had become.

The fourth time I went to service the Iranian, Ricardo told me the customer wanted something different. Instead of regular intercourse, he was demanding anal sex. I had never done that – and had never wanted to – and I pleaded with Ricardo not to make me do it. He told me not to be stupid, that it wasn't a big deal and – since the customer would pay extra – I just had to do what I was told.

I told the Iranian that this would be my first time, that I was afraid, and I asked him to be careful; to go slowly so that he didn't hurt me. That turned out to be a serious mistake. He gripped me roughly and forced his penis into my anus. The pain was excruciating and I cried out, begging him to stop, or at least to give my body a chance to relax enough to accommodate him. But my suffering just made him more aggressive and I realised that he was getting an extra kick out of hurting me. I buried my head in the pillow, trying to stifle my screams until he finished.

Afterwards, I could barely walk. But as we went to numb my agony with whisky, I understood that I had learned two lessons. The first was that for some men anal sex was not primarily about physical satisfaction but came from their need to dominate and degrade women. The second was that it was not safe to let them see how much pain it caused. What I didn't realise then was just how soon those lessons would become an inescapable part of my daily life.

For all the lies that Ricardo told us, one thing he was truthful about: he was running a business, and although I obviously never wanted to have sex with the Iranian, Ricardo did give me some of the money he received.

I know that many pimps – and that is exactly what Ricardo was – keep all the proceeds of their victim's sexual slavery. So why did he hand over some of the customer's cash – and why did I accept it? The first answer is easier than the second. Ricardo was calculating: he decided that sharing the money gave him an extra layer of control over me – essentially, he made me complicit in my own, repeated rape. Nor was the financial loss a hardship for him; Olivia discovered from talking to his friends that at the same time as he was selling me to the Iranian, he was pimping another girl – we never found out who – to other customers.

So why did I keep the money he thrust at me? That, I'm sorry to say, is more complicated and it doesn't paint us in a good light.

As we clung to each other, we talked – as naïve sixteen-year-olds do – of making a life together. At that point, of course, we had nowhere to go, but we dreamed, and, as the weeks and months ground on, our dreams grew bigger, more grandiose. We imagined ourselves far away from our village; sharing a warm and loving apartment of our own, safe from Ricardo's fists, and from the demands of the fat, sweaty Iranian.

As a first step, we put the earnings together with a little cash we had made working legitimately in a call centre and from cleaning our families' houses. But for our fantasy to become truly real, we knew we needed more money; and so we told ourselves that, for now, selling my body to Ricardo's customer was our only option.

How foolish we were. How childish our hopes must have seemed to Ricardo who overheard us discussing them one night. Certainly, he took full advantage. One afternoon, before our eighteenth birthdays, I was standing in my mother's kitchen when Olivia phoned me, her voice cracking with what sounded like fear. 'Ricardo has told me how he plans to make us all rich. As soon as we are eighteen, we can legally choose to work in prostitution. He says if we work in the Red Light District in Amsterdam, we can make a lot of money.'

I was horrified. 'No, no, no,' I told Olivia. 'It's not going to happen. I know he makes me have sex for money, but I'm not going to let you do this. And we aren't going to the Red Light District. Ever.'

Later that evening we all met up on the street as usual. Once again, Ricardo laid out his great scheme and insisted that it was the key to our fortunes. 'We are going to make a lot of money together: easy money, no problem. The Red Light District will make us all rich.'

I was appalled and disgusted. I stared at Ricardo, grinning with arrogant confidence in his power over us. I looked at Olivia, silently begging her to back me up and refuse to go along with this monstrous plan. I – we – should have said no; we certainly wanted to, and I had gone to the rendezvous with every intention of rejecting this latest demand. I don't know how it happened, but all my resolve dissolved. It's a measure of the total control over us that neither of us had the strength to refuse. I looked at Olivia, she looked at me, and with barely a word spoken we accepted our fate.

SIX

Olivia: Red Lights

We knew nothing: absolutely nothing.

Other than Anna's exploitation, which, terrible though it was, involved only one man, we had no understanding of what being a full-time prostitute actually involved. We barely even knew where the Red Light District was or how we would get there. We had only been there once, when we were twelve, and that was by mistake; neither of us could have found our own way back – at least not on our own.

Who would our customers be? Why would they pay us – two very young and, in our minds at least, not terribly attractive girls – for sex? How would we meet them? Was it safe – or even legal – for us to do this? Ricardo brushed all this aside.

'I know how the business works. Prostitution is perfectly legal in Amsterdam and I've made all the arrangements. It's not difficult: all you have to do is have sex with some people, and we'll all make a lot of money.'

He did admit that the Red Light District wasn't the safest place for two teenagers, which was why we needed him. 'I will protect you; I'll be like your manager and handle all the business side of the venture. You don't need to worry about anything.'

He made everything sound so simple. He would do all the difficult work: all we had to do was to take the customers' money – in return for the 'easy' job of lying down and letting them fuck us.

I write these words as a thirty-three-year-old woman. I look back at my seventeen-year-old self and think, why? Why did we let Ricardo do this to us? Why, how, could we agree to something so obscene? Why didn't we say no? I shake my head – I know the answer. Ricardo had carefully prepared us for exactly this moment, by befriending us, paying us attention and taking us out drinking. There is a word for that process today – grooming – but back in 2003, as far as I know it hadn't been invented. And he had moved from grooming onto the next stage: brutal, unpredictable violence. It had enabled him to force Anna to service his Iranian client for two full years, and it was ultimately the reason we couldn't say no to the final step in the scheme. So, though we were naïve, foolish and sometimes irresponsible, the thing I am sure of is that we never actually agreed to become full-time prostitutes because we simply didn't have the power to say 'no'.

Did Ricardo really plan all of this? Yes. Yes, he did. He was deliberate, patient and manipulative, and two things above all proved that he had set out to exploit us from the beginning.

The first was that soon after he dropped his bombshell, gossip went around our village that we were going to work for him as prostitutes in Amsterdam. My sister heard these stories and quickly told my parents. My relationship with my mum and dad had almost completely broken down by this point, but to their credit they tracked down the address of Ricardo's girlfriend's apartment and went over there to confront him. It says something about his brazen confidence that he wasn't flustered or even embarrassed. He admitted the rumours they had heard were true, but told them that Anna and I had come up with the whole idea of prostitution and selling ourselves in the Red Light District; he was only involved because it was 'very dangerous out there', and he had kindly offered us his protection.

No, my parents didn't fall for this. Nor did Anna's. But neither of them made any attempt to oppose Ricardo, much less to prevent him prostituting us. Instead, they took out their disgust on us. They told us in no uncertain terms that we should not, must not do this; they told us we couldn't live in their houses if we 'chose' to become prostitutes. Anna's father was particularly angry and particularly blunt: he said, 'I didn't put a whore in the cradle,' and gave her a month to move out of his home. My family made it clear that the same ultimatum applied to me.

But Ricardo saw that coming; he simply rented, suspiciously quickly, an apartment for us both – on condition, of course, that the cost would be deducted from our share of the money we earned as prostitutes. And that was that: we calmly said goodbye to our families and to the last vestiges of our old lives.

Could we have done more to ask for our families' protection? I don't believe so. We were then completely under Ricardo's control – beaten and brutalised into submission. And I also think in the end that our parents were relieved to see us go; they were so caught up in their own personal struggles and needs, and our behaviour had become so difficult, that they no longer had the time, strength or patience for their children. And, if I am to be truly honest, by that time we didn't really care either.

The second reason I am sure Ricardo had planned our transition from schoolgirls to sex workers were the fundamental changes that had taken place in Holland's prostitution laws. These had come into force at almost exactly the same time as he first sold Anna to his customer and, coupled with further 'reforms', introduced just before he announced our new business venture, they made it much easier – and much safer – for him to pimp us.

We knew nothing about any of this. But he did, and our situation was worsened by the Dutch attitude to prostitution and, even more so, our country's inability to protect the women who are traded at the heart of its capital's centre.

Dutch postcode 1012 is a surprisingly small place – just 1.6 acres in total. It includes twenty main streets, from which a much larger maze of little alleys branch out, cutting through to the network of canals which form its real borders. But its main selling point is its position: right slap bang in the heart of Amsterdam, a conveniently short walk from the central train station and almost impossible for tourists heading to the city's other attractions to miss. This is the district known officially as De Wallen, but more usually called *de Rosse Buurt*: The Red Light District.

There is a long history of prostitution there but it was in the early 1970s, during the sexual revolution, that Amsterdam – and De Wallen in particular – was able to cash in on the boom in commercial sex tourism. Neon-lit 'windows' – small rooms with a large plate-glass frontage and a red light outside – sprouted along this network of alleys, each with a half-naked woman offering cheap, 'easy' sex. Ever since, customers have flocked from all over the world to take advantage of these women's bodies, along with the porn shops, live sex shows and 'coffeeshops' that make up the garish life of this district.

But it was not just the former local Dutch customers, who had long sidled into its alleys in search of quick and rubber-clad relief, who came to the district, but plane after plane full of international sex tourists, in search of a quick thrill – or rather a succession of thrills. Weekend stag parties of young men with cash to splash; sad older men, who relished the chance to fuck youthful girls they could no longer attract unaided by money; fetishists, drawn by my country's relaxed attitude towards exceptional sexual tastes; and among all of these, normal men and women – holidaymakers who found time in their tour schedules to stop off and experience the kick of being in and around such shameless, naked carnality.

None of this was legitimate or above board. In theory, prostitution was against the law; the windows and the more upscale brothels, which soon sprung up beside them, were officially outlawed and pimping was a serious criminal offence. But, just as with the equally illegal weed, Holland managed to turn a blind eye; the government refused to legalise the sale of sex or drugs, but adopted a policy of not enforcing the laws on its statute books. There was a reason for this: money.

The financial benefits of the vice trade – as it was some-times still quaintly called – were enormous. Millions of British pounds, American dollars, French francs and Japanese yen rolled into the coffers of Amsterdam's city council every year, and within a short time the sex trade became one of the pillars of the local economy. But what started as an additional income stream soon grew, like a tumour invading a patient, to the point at which it took over the body politic. As the dawn of the new millennium approached, there were an estimated 25,000 sex workers operating across the country, and prostitution paid the wages of thousands of ordinary people.

Finally, in 1998, Holland gave up the fight and effectively sanctioned the commercial sex trade. Under a new law, prostitution was formally recognised as a 'profession' in Holland. Two years later, brothels were decriminalised and it became perfectly legal for one human being to pimp another, providing there was no coercion or violence involved. Cities like Amsterdam were given the power to licence and – again, in theory – regulate the trade in women's bodies.

The justification for this reform was not simply economic. Money – especially such vast amounts, all of it in cash – had attracted serious organized crime. International gangs trafficked women into the Red Light District from South America, Africa and – especially – from the remnants of the former Soviet Union, forcing them to service the insatiable demands of sex tourism. Pimps took over De Wallen, ruling its network of alleys and windows with extreme violence. Drugs, too, flowed in; heroin, cocaine and ecstasy became as prominent – and as openly available – as weed. The once-pretty streets lining the canals became ever more sordid and dangerous.

It was to combat this rise in trafficking, and the gangs of violent pimps and associated dealers, that the new laws were introduced. The idea was that if individual women were allowed to sell sex without fear of arrest, then somehow the international sex slavery and organized crime syndicates which traded women's unwilling bodies across international borders would magically disappear. And so from early in 2000 – exactly at the moment that Ricardo first latched on to Anna and I – any woman over the age of eighteen who held a European Union passport was given the right to set herself up in business, to rent a room in which to sell her body and operate just like any other self-employed trader. She could even, if she chose to, work for an 'employer', or pimp, whose activities were henceforth entirely legal. To ensure the safety of these 'Happy Hookers', the city council was given power to licence Red Light District windows, charging a fee and requiring the owner of the buildings to install panic buttons in every room used for prostitution. Local police units were also instructed to patrol De Wallen, keeping a watchful eye on this newly regulated production line of sex.

I don't believe the timing was a coincidence. I am certain that Ricardo saw in this new era of legal pimping an opportunity – and Anna and I were to be his meal ticket. Once he found us and began the process of successfully grooming us, there were only two slight obstacles in his path. The first was that the Red Light District was still controlled by violent international gangs – mostly from Turkey or the former Balkan Republics; stepping on to their turf would need careful preparation and making full use of the new rules regulating the renting of windows. The second was our age. The police and government had – somewhat belatedly – realised that sex tourists were being drawn to Amsterdam by an increase in the number of under-age girls sold by their pimps. Most were sixteen (though some were younger), and the new licensing system was specifically designed to put an end to this trade in children; it imposed a strict requirement that any girl applying for a permit to set up in business as a prostitute had to be at least eighteen years old, and required her to present documentary proof in the form of a passport or other official identity document at the real estate office which rented out Red Light District windows.

Ricardo knew this. He worked out that in our little village, he could get away undetected with forcing Anna and his other victim to sell themselves to a single customer at a time, but the world's shop window of the commercial flesh trade was a very much more visible proposition; he knew he needed to wait until we reached the magical age of sexual adulthood.

In any case, this gave him the time – as well as the money – to groom, intimidate and overwhelm us so completely that when he announced that our 'partnership' would be launched on our eighteenth birthdays – Anna first, me exactly one week later – we would be powerless to refuse.

This, then, was the new world we were about to inhabit: the theoretically licensed, controlled 'safe space' for commercial sex. We were to join the thousands of prostitutes working, willingly or otherwise, behind the neon-lit glass of 300 windows in the Red Light District. Whereas most girls celebrate their eighteenth birthdays with a party, a night out or a family dinner, we were about to learn the price of Amsterdam's new policy of tolerance and legalisation: '€50 suck and a fuck'.

SEVEN

Anna: Adult

Reach out. Stretch my arms wide – the tips of my fingers can almost touch the walls on either side of this box.

The walls are bare. No pictures or photographs decorate the stretches of what was – once – white plaster. Now it is a faded shade of dirty yellow, varnished to a grubby, dull sheen from absorbing years of cigarette smoke and nicotine. The floor is cold and tiled. There are tiny cracks in the filthy grey grout between them. An unwanted thought: won't they attract germs and provide a safe place for bacteria to flourish?

There is no furniture in this room save a little stool and a narrow, single bed, covered in worn red plastic (also slightly cracked). No sheet. No pillow. No cover. Nothing that makes it a bed; instead it's just a table. Beside it there is a plastic bucket with a lid perched on top; it shows the marks of repeated heavy use.

At the front, the sheet glass window is covered by dusty red curtains. At the back, a plain, cheap door leads to a dingy corridor running the length of the building; plastic bags, stuffed with kitchen roll, detergent and commercial-size boxes of industrial-strength condoms, for now still in their in shiny foil packets, lean at drunken angles against the length of the skirting. Further down there is a small, surprisingly clean toilet and wash basin.

Look around. These four walls confining me are a space from which all traces of humanity have been removed. No, not removed – they were never here. This is a room of *business*: a narrow, stark rectangle where the sole interaction between those within is transactional. And impersonal.

This room is not quiet. Beside it, spreading out along this terraced row of what once were smart seventeenth-century canal-side homes, are other similar cubicles, each identically furnished – if that's the right word – and each containing someone like me. I hear the creak of their table beds and the regular snap of bucket lids, catch the rattle of drapes drawn back and forth, sense them – my colleagues, my co-workers, my fellow inmates – displaying themselves to the world outside.

The din from the night streets – the laughter of happy, rowdy revellers; shouts and football chants from groups of young men emboldened by beer, and the steady beat of foot-steps on the cobbles – filters through the plate-glass window at the front of my box.

6.55 p.m. Five minutes to seven – 300 seconds before my life changes for ever. I try to count them. I fail.

7 p.m. Time. I shuffle to the front of this little space, grasp the curtains in both hands, shut my eyes and draw them open. When I unclench my eyes, I am no longer Anna Hendriks, only child of a once-safe and happy family in a quiet Dutch village.

Now I am nameless, a no one, something to be bought, used and forgotten. I am a chattel, a disposable tool; invisible yet simultaneously on full show. I am now a full-time prostitute in the Red Light District of Amsterdam. I am shaking, terrified and alone; I am also blind drunk.

Today is my eighteenth birthday.

Ricardo took us to Amsterdam. He picked us up in an unlicensed taxi from the village at lunchtime and we all headed, in total silence, up the motorway which leads to the heart of the city centre. Olivia and I were completely numb; our minds could not process what we knew would shortly be done to my body. And so we didn't speak; we simply could not.

We parked up on a side street and he gestured us towards a nondescript building, somewhere off the main streets winding through De Wallen. This, he explained, was the premises of the agency licensed by the city council to rent out window rooms in the Red Light District, and the first rung on the ladder of our brave new business venture.

Ricardo, though, was evidently not that brave – or, at least, he was cautious for his own security. Although pimping was now legal – assuming a prostitute chose freely and willingly to avail herself of this breed of 'employer' – his presence and my near-catatonic state might raise suspicions that I had been coerced into selling my body. And so he lounged in the car, sending Olivia and I into the office to tell lies to the bureaucracy of the sex trade about our 'voluntary' determination to work in the neon-lit windows.

A middle-aged Indonesian man sat behind a plain desk. Ricardo had evidently called earlier, warning him to expect me, and he showed no emotion when I told him I wanted to rent a room, to set myself up as an independent prostitute, responsible for my own safety, welfare, health care and taxes. I pointed at Olivia and explained that she wanted to do the same. I stressed, as Ricardo had ordered, that we had reached this decision on our own, that we had not been subjected to any physical force and that we were perfectly happy about our choice of new career. Lies, all lies; not that it mattered. The agency official asked only one question: were we eighteen?

I'm setting out the detail of this tedious administrative process because it seems – with hindsight – so bizarrely banal and yet so fundamentally important. There were then around 300 sex windows licensed by the council in the Red Light District (no one then knew exactly how many), and between one and three thousand (mostly) women who chose to enter them every year.

Legalised prostitution and the licensing scheme itself had been established because of solid evidence that victims were being trafficked and forced to work there by violent criminal gangs. And yet the single – the only – question we were asked was whether, under the new laws, we were of the required legal age and entitled to choose this line of business. Not once did the man given the responsibility for renting out premises – the gatekeeper of the whole industry – ask whether we really wanted to lie down and be fucked for a living. Not once.

Ricardo knew it would be like this. I didn't know if he had previously sent other girls like us to this office, each primed with his sorry little lies, but he knew how the system worked; he knew that very well. And so I pulled my passport out of my pocket, showed it to the official as proof that I had, indeed, attained the magic age of eighteen years – in fact, I'd done so that very morning – and explained that on Olivia's birthday, just over one week from now, she would be returning to repeat the performance. The man shrugged, turned away, and pulled out a sheaf of closely typed forms from a drawer in the desk: the rental agreement, with the terms and conditions of my impending bondage set out in a professionally printed contract. He told me that the windows operated on an eighteen-hour business day, split into two shifts – day and night – and asked which did I want? I was ready for the question; once again, Ricardo had coached me well and I picked the second, more profitable, period. My new office hours would be 7 p.m. to 4 a.m. (finishing an hour later on weekends), and I was given the strong impression that, in some odd eruption of civic pride, Amsterdam expected me to be in place and available throughout my shift.

For the privilege of selling my body in its licenced space, I solemnly undertook to pay the agency's standard rate for the shift rental – €100 per night, six nights every week – I promised to keep the place clean and tidy, and to be responsible for my own bodily checks and welfare. The agency might take a cut for licensing my prison to me, and feel it was important that my window never went dark through dereliction of duty, but it seemed the city council had no interest in ensuring I did not succumb to sexually transmitted infections. That was to be my concern – just one of the costs of choosing to operate my business. I signed the agreement.

I must, though, give the agency clerk some credit for what he did next. He realised that this was my first time in the Red Light District, saw that I was new to the industry and – I think – sensed the truth that I was not in any way doing this of my own free will. None of this stopped him from issuing a contract to an evidently terrified and only barely legal girl to sell her body – so he can't have cared that much – but he stood up and announced that he would take me to my window himself. Since this was evidently a kindness he didn't generally offer to the agency's other customers, it was apparent that in some way I was being given the easiest introduction he could provide.

The room was on *Oudezijds Achterburtgwal* – the long street and adjacent canal running through the heart of De Wallen. Once the eastern border of the historic city (and, with a certain bitter aptness, the location of a medieval women's prison), by April 2003 it had been split laterally into two distinct halves. Bridge number 215 marked the dividing line between the southern and respectable part, occupied by faculties of the University of Amsterdam, and the noisy northern end where coffeeshops, strip clubs, brothels and – above all else – the famous red-light windows drew thousands of visitors every single night of the year. We pushed through the afternoon crowds, found the one assigned to me, next door to a live sex show called *SexPalace*, and – another first, apparently – the agency guy then introduced me to the women in the next-door cubicles, telling them 'this is a new girl, show her how things work'.

They did. They told me the cheapest place to buy the supplies I would shortly need – the rolls of paper tissues, detergent, giant boxes of condoms; they pointed out the panic button which would – in theory – summon help if I encountered trouble. And then, initiation over, they went back to the business of enticing customers into to their own windows. Olivia and I looked at each other, the full weight of what lay ahead finally hitting us. I began to shiver.

When Ricardo showed up his instructions were direct and evidently uncomplicated by fear – at least for him – of what my job involved. The first and most fundamental rule was that I was here to work, to earn money for us all, and that therefore the harder I worked, the richer we would all become. He didn't need to elaborate what hard work meant: as many customers as I could accommodate, as briefly as I could get away with, for as much money as I could extract from their wallets.

There was, though, a set price list – and one to which I was expected to adhere without deviation. A standard session was fifteen minutes; each customer was to be lured inside my window with the promise of a suck and fuck for the basic fee of €50, always paid up front. If the man didn't – or couldn't – finish in the allotted time, that was his problem, not mine. I was to tell him either to pull up his pants and leave or – the better alternative, according to Ricardo – to fork out another €50 for an extra 15 minutes.

Other even more profitable options were on my menu of services. Customers requesting a full hour were to be relieved immediately of €250. I wondered, briefly, what could take them that long; surely they wouldn't be able to spend all that time inside me? Ricardo helpfully explained. Different positions were a valuable extra at €20 each (in addition to the extra time fees), as were demands for me to remove items of clothing; the entry-level session involved me retaining my bra and panties – taking either off would cost the customer another €20 or, if he seemed gullible, €50. Ricardo made it all sound like being a taxi driver, with an initial call-out charge and every half-kilometre thereafter calibrated and carefully metered. I thought: 'That's easy for you to say, because in this line of work the vehicle being rented out is my body, not yours.' But, of course, I was too scared to say this to his face.

Orders duly issued, Ricardo sloped off to a nearby bar from which – so he assured me – he would be keeping a protective eye on my window. He would come and pick me up at the end of my shift, at which point we were to share out the earnings.

Olivia and I went to buy supplies. To the assortment of cleaning products, tissues and rubber sheaths we added packs of cigarettes and a large bottle of whisky and several cans of Red Bull. The booze was the most urgent priority: I knew I could not do this sober – and there was very little time to get properly drunk.

A little before 7 p.m. Olivia had to leave – the Red Light District rules about her age meant that she was not allowed to be with me in the window. I hated watching her go; I felt desperately alone and, as I began to prepare for my night's work, utterly terrified. The women in the neighbouring rooms were all heavily made up and dressed – or half dressed – in skimpy lingerie. To comply with Ricardo's demands for a prof-itable shift, it dawned on me that I was supposed to compete with them for customers; a few hours ago, they had tried to teach me the basics of the sex trade, but now they were my rivals. I realised that I should change into underwear which, like theirs, teased and provoked, and cover my face with similarly alluring swathes of make-up: dark shadow above my eyes, a gaudy slash of bright red lipstick to emphasise my availability. But I couldn't.

I had always been horribly insecure about my appearance; I was very skinny and didn't have any adult female curves – the very features I was meant to display. No matter what it said in my passport, I knew that really I looked like a child of around fourteen or fifteen. Even if I had the confidence to do so, I couldn't see how it was possible to change the juvenile appearance of my face – let alone my body – with the tricks and trappings of an adult woman. And so I listlessly applied a few smears of make-up before facing up to what I should wear. Olivia and I had discussed this and because I told her I didn't want to expose any more of my body than I absolutely had to, she had lent me a very long black sleeveless dress. I pulled it over my head, saw that it came almost down to my ankles and that its looseness made me seem as if I was wearing the sort of shapeless *burqa* women in Muslim communities use to conceal their frames – and their sexuality – from the eyes of men.

I knew, of course, that this wasn't appropriate attire for someone working in the windows, but I told myself that – for tonight at least – it would protect me from the most aggressive and demanding customers. I couldn't have been more wrong.

A few minutes after I pulled back the curtain, my first customer knocked on the window. He was an older man, around the same age as Ricardo's Iranian, so I suppose it shouldn't have been a surprise that he wanted to rent the body of someone young enough to be his daughter, but somehow it was. I can't honestly remember what exactly he said or how long he stayed – my mind has blocked most of those details – just that he handed over his €50 and, after rolling a condom onto his penis, I took him as briefly as possible in my mouth and then lay back while he penetrated me. When he was done he left without, as far as I can recall, a single word.

Over. It was over. My first customer as a full-time window prostitute. I reached for the whisky, the Red Bull, cigarettes – and my phone. As much as I craved a numbing shot of alcohol and the soothing pull of nicotine into my lungs, my most urgent need was Olivia; I had to hear her voice, and feel the warmth of her love for me as I told her that it was done and I was safe. And almost all of that happened. Almost.

She was in a nearby bar with Ricardo, watching him down shots of Hennessy brandy – his contribution, apparently, to our business. She picked up almost immediately and we managed a few snatched words. But I was wrong about the most important thing I had to tell her, because it wasn't over – not this night, let alone those that stretched endlessly ahead; not by a long way.

I opened the curtain again, sat down on the stool – I found I didn't have the strength or the confidence to stand and pose like the women in the neighbouring rooms – and looked out at the people pacing up and down *Achterburtgwal*. There were a remarkably large number of them, but whilst some were peering in the windows on either side of mine, inspecting their prospective purchases and beginning the negotiations that would lead them inside, there seemed to be a small group of men starting to form up outside my window. Why were they standing there? They weren't lining up beside any other red light – so why was mine so apparently popular? How naïve I was.

Over the next seven hours I had the answer forced inside me. Repeatedly. Customer after customer banged on my glass – some had evidently waited in line, or gone off for a drink while I serviced someone else – and the majority of them made it clear why I was so popular: because I looked so young.

It had never occurred to me before that there are a lot of dirty old men, quasi-paedophiles really, who were aroused by the idea of having sex with someone who looked like a child; nor that the Red Light District enabled them to indulge this particular fetish without fear of police attention or hostile public opinion. All they had to do was turn up, pay up and fantasise that the little body they were renting was under the age of consent.

Most of these clients were middle-aged. Some of them were old enough to be my grandfather. For the first time that night a powerful, unstoppable emotion punctuated the haze of booze in which my mind floated. It was disgusting. They were disgusting. And I was disgusting, too – why? Because my inability to paint my face or to pose and preen in adult clothing had reinforced the illusion, enabled their fetish. In trying to hide the evidence of my real age, I had made myself seem even more childlike.

That night some genuine tourists, who had no interest in coming inside my window, made a point of stopping to ask how old I was. They told me they thought I was fifteen; even some of my customers questioned whether I was old enough to be in that window. They didn't, though, challenge me when I told them I was eighteen; it seemed that they were simply relieved that what they wanted from me was legal.

By four o' clock the next morning I had lost count of the number of customers – eight? ten? – who had paid to have sex with me. There was a stack of euros in my purse and the bin was stuffed with used condoms and dirty paper towels, but I didn't have the strength or the heart to count either. I only knew that my body ached terribly and inside and out felt red-raw.

If my body was broken, my mind was worse. All faint traces of self-esteem that I possessed were as shattered as my body. I felt abused, dirty and despite the money – more than €400 – balled up in my bag, waiting for Ricardo to collect, I felt utterly worthless. I had spent the last hours of my birthday, and the first few of the morning after, as a prostitute. And I would do so again tomorrow; and the next day, and all the days from there on in. This, now, was my life.

EIGHT

Olivia: Cost

On my eighteenth birthday I got up at 11 a.m., showered, dressed and ran through the menial chores of washing clothes and cleaning the house. I had not slept well; I had tried, in vain, to block out what I knew was coming, but fear and revulsion constantly invaded my thoughts and kept me awake. Going through the routine of a normal existence was my way of trying to stop my mind from churning. I made the jobs last until around 4 p.m., then Anna and I ate before gathering what we would need for the night ahead: snacks, drinks and the supplies of our trade.

Ricardo turned up an hour later, pushed us into the back of an unlicensed taxi, and lounged in the front, music blaring to stop any chance of conversation, as it drove us to Amsterdam. He dropped us off at *Nieuwmarkt*, a large square in the city's Chinatown, just behind the Red Light District; from here Anna and I walked through the maze of alleys to the rental office where we were to collect our room keys.

The same Indonesian man was behind the desk. As with Anna, he asked for proof that I was of legal age to sell my body, then briefly talked me through the contract for my window. Perhaps because Anna was with me, he didn't offer to show me where I would be working; his limited interest in me as a human being ended once the agreement was signed. We left the agency and plodded back through the cobbled streets to *Achterburgwal*. Our bags, heavy with detergent, tissues and condoms, were slung over our shoulders; they seemed horribly large – a visible sign of shame that marked us out to the commuters making their way home and to the crowds of tourists jammed into the narrow lanes. I felt utterly, wretchedly humiliated and, as each step took me closer to my new workplace, closer to the moment when I would have to surrender my body to the demands of strangers, I felt a growing, debilitating terror.

My window was next to Anna's; that, at least, was some comfort since it would allow us to keep an eye on each other and meant we could – assuming our night's schedule allowed – meet up between customers to smoke and drink. The latter, I knew, was my only hope of getting through this, and as soon as we got inside, we filled large glasses with whisky and Red Bull. But no matter how many slugs of soothing alcohol I swallowed, I found I could not face up to getting undressed. I just could not bring myself to strip down to my underwear, knowing that the moment I did so I was crossing a threshold from which I could never pass back. Dressed, I was still Olivia Smit; in my bra and pants I was a prostitute, a nameless €50 whore.

Ricardo turned up. In desperation I found the strength to beg him not to make me sell myself: 'I cannot do this. I can't – I really can't. Please, please don't make me.' It made no difference: he grabbed my arm and told me, coldly and forcefully: 'You will do this. You have no choice. Now, get ready.' I tried to reason with him again, then I refused outright. He hit me. Over and over again, slapping and punching me in the stomach and ribs – he was careful not to mark my face – threatening me and then threatening Anna. I heard a voice screaming and sobbing and it took a few seconds before I realised that it was mine. Then Ricardo pushed me away from him, walked to the door and stepped out into the street. And that was that. Resistance finished. Old life over.

I stripped and sat down on the stool beside the bed. Then, at 7 p.m. precisely, I drew back the curtains and looked out on the street, peering and trying to spot which of the men passing by would be my first customer. It was raining, one of those dank spring nights in which the water on the cobbles and the sluggish canal beside them reflected the neon glare back on the glass. I was cold, shivering and as drunk as possible. I was absolutely terrified.

Strange as this will sound, there was an additional and very particular aspect to my fear. I had never had sex with a white man before, and for some unfathomable reason, the prospect of doing so – of having to do so, with a succession of them and for money – made everything even more overwhelming.

As it turned out, my very first client – he turned up half an hour after I pulled back the curtains – was black, his body as dark as Ricardo's, and around the same age. In some way this helped – the mind finds what comfort and protection it can, I suppose. Please don't misunderstand: it was not easy to let him through the door, and I very definitely did not want to do so, but the faint trace of ethnic familiarity made it fractionally less difficult than it would otherwise have been.

He was brisk – matter-of-fact, really – about what he wanted. '15 minutes – €50 suck and fuck' was what I had offered, and that's exactly what he chose. I pulled the drapes closed and, as he dropped his pants and boxer shorts, I took up the tools of my new trade. I sanitised his genitals with an alcohol-infused wipe, clumsily unrolled a condom over his penis and perched on the bed to take him into my mouth. A few minutes later I stood up, turned round and bent over so that I wouldn't have to see his face.

Every woman working in the windows develops her own technique. I hope I don't need to say that this isn't for any satisfaction she might gain from her work; take it from me that the myth of sex workers deriving any pleasure from their labour is just that – a myth. Instead, it's a way of coping with the act itself, and with the psychological cost of allowing a complete stranger inside their bodies.

Anna and I had talked about how she placed herself – always in the missionary position, always straining to keep as much of the customer's skin off her own as was physically possible. I knew this would be impossible for me. I couldn't bear the idea of seeing the clients' faces as they groaned and grunted above me – and it felt neither safe nor practical to keep my eyes clenched tightly shut throughout the allotted fifteen minutes. If they paid to change position, well, that would be a bridge to cross later, but I was determined at least to start by facing away.

The man entered me, doggy-style. His hands gripped my legs. He thrust. He bucked. He finished. I pulled away, grabbed a wad of kitchen roll and pulled the used condom off him, dropping it as quickly as I could in the bin. He left. It was done. I was now a prostitute.

I wanted to look for Anna, to hear her voice, tell her I was okay. But a client had come to her window and I knew better than to interrupt; Ricardo would be lurking somewhere in a nearby bar, watching the passing foot traffic, checking that we weren't slacking; his mind would be calculating his earnings as diligently as he measured out the shots of expensive brandy that sustained his night's 'work'. He would not tolerate any unnecessary breaks in our service. Not without violence.

So I turned to my own nourishment, slipped a cigarette out of the pack, inhaled the smoke as deeply as I could, then took a substantial hit of whisky. The alcohol served two purposes: it led me deeper into the well of numbness and simultaneously sterilised my mouth. I didn't want to think what had just been inside there – let alone further down – but I had to.

I drew the curtains closed, and began cleaning my body with a sanitising tissue. As I went through this ritual – the first time I would do so, but not the last, I knew – I began to wonder about the man who had just left. Who was he? Why had he come here? What made him think it was okay to penetrate my body, just because he had the cash to make it legal? I realised I had no idea. I didn't know his name, where he was from, what he did for a living. I had no information about his family, his background or what he had been thinking while he fucked me. He was a complete and total stranger, and yet he had just done the most intimate thing a man can do with a woman.

And then, even though my mind was dulled by booze, I saw that this was not true. There had been no such intimacy, not even the merest hint of it. Intimacy involved tenderness –

or, at the very least, communication; there had been neither. And did not intimacy entail – surely it *required* – a genuine and mutual consent? Even the quickest, sleaziest hook-up or one-night stand came with these essential components; yet just now they had been notable by their absence, business substituting for emotion and willingness. Kissing was off-limits, completely out of the question, but at least – and forgive me if this now sounds too sentimental for the room I then occupied – true intimacy should absolutely include some moments of voluntary touching? I re-played the fifteen-minute suck and fuck in my mind; I saw myself shrink from the man's hands and body, trying to keep my skin away from his.

No. There was no intimacy in this sad little drama we had just enacted. There was commerce, industry and effort; a transaction, nothing more and nothing less – assuming you accepted the lie that it was an honest and voluntary exchange of services for payment. I had no clue what the customer had gained from it other than some temporary sexual relief. And me? In this brave new world of prostitution – legal and safe by an act of parliament – had I gained or lost? Yes, I would get half of the fee – minus, of course, the price of renting this room and the supplies I needed – but how high would the mental cost of this share turn out to be?

Which is when it hit me, again. I had completed less than ten per cent of a nine-hour shift – I had serviced just one client. I had eight hours, and God knows how many customers, still ahead of me. And that was just tonight; the rest of this life – my life now – stretched on into the impossible distance, with no break or relief in sight. It was a viciously sobering thought. I decided to get more drunk.

Anna was there before me. Physically, she had been in the windows a whole week longer, had been fucked by at least fifty strangers, and wiped herself clean – or at least as clean as possible – afterwards. Mentally, she was now much, much older than I; the childhood friend with whom I had shared everything as an equal, a co-conspirator in our mutual misery, had gone ahead of me into a place so dark and damaging that her eyes had begun to take on what battle-fatigued soldiers call 'the thousand-yard stare'. I was following her, but she was already there. It was hardly a surprise, then, that when I eventually found her later that night, somewhere in the bowels of that old building on the cobbles of *Achterburgwal*, she had passed out from all the booze she had swallowed. I woke her, sat her up and eventually got some food and water down her throat. Then we went back to work.

I would like to tell you that the night got easier. That would be the Hollywood movie version of how things played out – *Pretty Woman* set beside Amsterdam's canals. I can't; it didn't. The rest of my customers – I serviced another five over the next eight hours – did not match up even to the limited standard of the first. They were white, they were older, and they felt consecutively worse. Each was much harder to accommodate than the first man; each act of penetration was much more traumatic for me to process than the one who preceded him. In the end they formed an unforgiving and largely silent line – at least in my mind – of utter hopelessness. Mine, theirs, the whole damn world's; that's how it felt because that's how it was.

Yet even in this bleak and pitiless landscape, I had found time to think. And what struck me was so random, so frankly absurd, that I almost – almost – found myself laughing out loud. Not one of the men who knocked on my window, entered my room, paid to enter me, appeared to have any understanding of the price they had paid; I don't mean the cost to me (or even them, assuming there was one), but the actual financial outlay they had just expended. Each had handed over their €50 without seeming to give it much thought. Did this mean that they had such a large amount of disposable income that they didn't need to calculate the value in terms of price per minute – something which, given their less than glamorous appearance, didn't seem likely? Or was it that their needs were so overwhelming – and that it was me who was so disposable – that the question never even crossed their minds?

In the end, I realised that something else was at play. In April 2003, the euro was still a relatively new currency for Holland; my country had dropped its old banknote – the guilder – in favour of the new money just over a year earlier, and people had still not fully appreciated the exchange rate which calculated the value of the true value of the euros in their wallet. It had allowed the commercial sex trade to inflate the prices of women like me without anyone really noticing. It seemed an apt metaphor for the whole sordid business.

At 4 a.m. Ricardo appeared at the windows to collect Anna and I, and – naturally – to assess his profits. Between us we had amassed a stash of almost €1000; his cut was half of these earnings – and he didn't have to worry about any overheads, since these all fell on our exhausted shoulders. He was, unsurprisingly, perfectly happy.

I, by contrast, was dog-tired, drunk – with the early harbingers of a sickening hangover – and terribly, hatefully sore.

Every part of my body ached; I felt filthy. As soon as I got back to the apartment, I ran into the shower, desperate to wash away the dirt of the night. I scrubbed at my face, my arms, legs, feet and genitals, but no matter how hard I worked I couldn't rid myself of the sensation that every pore on my skin remained clogged with grime; nor could the soap cleanse the shame and humiliation polluting my mind.

I fell into bed, drained and drunk, but was unable to go to sleep. I found myself trying to recall the faces of the men who I'd serviced but my mind stubbornly refused to summon up their features. For some reason, this made everything worse.

So I ended the first night of my life as a Red Light District prostitute lying exhausted but sleepless, tormented by what had been done to my body and by the unnerving sensation that my mind was beginning to break free of my control. This was the true cost of prostitution, and it was paid not by the customers but by me and Anna and by all the other women in the windows. And I saw with horrible clarity that I – we – were to pay this price, night after night, week after week, years without end.

Only one thing interrupted this brutal cycle – and then only temporarily. Four weeks after I started work – after 24 nights, 54 hours and, as best as I could calculate, after having been fucked by almost 200 men – I stopped.

My respite from sex was not voluntary, though, but since I was exhausted and never wanted to see the inside of the Red Light District again, I was quite thankful. Nor was it complete or without danger, but instead forced upon me and – to his evident annoyance – on Ricardo. Because one month after I turned eighteen, I discovered I was pregnant.

I'd thought something was wrong for a little while, but in the weeks leading up to my birthday I had assumed that it was just my mind reacting to the stress of what Anna and I were about to be made to do; so I ignored the rumblings in my stomach and the early feelings of sickness until they became too strong to disregard. When I finally took the test, it turned out that I was seven weeks gone; for more than half of that period I had opened my legs for a succession of men.

There was never any question about the identity of the baby's father. From the moment he got his claws into us, to the night I began work as a prostitute, Ricardo was the only person with whom I had sex. His violent possessiveness had ensured that, if nothing else, there could never be any doubt that he was responsible for the foetus growing inside me.

I wasn't, though, sure how it could have happened. Like Anna, I was on the pill (Ricardo made it plain that he wouldn't ever use a condom) and I was very careful indeed to ensure I never missed a single day's tablet. Perhaps the antibiotics from the chlamydia infection had caused the pill to fail. Whatever the cause, the little test kit told me the result. I was now nearly two months pregnant.

I confided in Anna straight away and together we agreed that there was no way to keep this from Ricardo. No matter what I chose to do about the situation, he would have to know. I plucked up the courage to tell him on the way back from our shift in the windows; his reaction was all I should have expected. 'You're not going to keep this, right? I already have a child; I don't need another one.'

He was, of course, right. Selfish, yes, and heartless too, but deadly accurate about the impossibility of me going through with the pregnancy. I remembered what had happened when his girlfriend found out we had been having sex. I remembered the punishment beating Ricardo doled out, the gun he forced into my mouth, and knew that I dared not risk that again – this time his finger might not pull back from the trigger.

Beyond that, unspoken because there was simply no way to discuss it with him, was the stark assumption that I couldn't carry on working in the windows if I kept the baby.

Although Anna and I had already encountered some truly strange customers and dealt with their demands for the most bizarre fetishes, they were – then – a small minority; the likelihood of me attracting a substantial number of men who wanted to fuck a heavily pregnant girl was remote. And Ricardo had made one thing very plain from the beginning: volume was the key to our 'success'. I knew almost as soon as I saw the test result that I could not – would not – keep this baby. It was simply not an option.

But I must also be honest. I didn't want to go through with the pregnancy anyway; I could not imagine myself as a mother because I knew deep down that I was still a child myself. I might be doing the most adult job a woman can perform, but that was just my body; my head, my mind, were still adolescent.

Yet at the same time, I do not want to mislead you; I do not believe any woman contemplates an abortion without some flicker of unease. However rational the choice, however much a termination is the right, sensible and responsible decision to make – somewhere, deep down in all of us, there is still a vestigial sense of sorrow and loss.

Despite my family's rejection of me, I'd stayed in touch with my sister. After the five-day 'cooling off' period required by Dutch law, she took me to the clinic – a facility on the east side of Amsterdam, some distance from De Wallen and from my old village – and stayed with me throughout the day while I had my termination. When it was time to leave, she drove me back to the apartment I shared with Anna.

I was bleeding heavily and the doctor had given me firm instructions not to have sex until a month after the abortion. That obviously meant I could not go straight back to the windows. Not surprisingly, this did not please Ricardo, who saw it as an inconvenient interruption to the substantial sums of money he was 'earning' from my body. Nor was he willing to defer his own sexual demands; just seven days after the termination he insisted on fucking me again. And a fortnight after that he told me – forcefully – it was time to go back to work. My brief respite was over. I was taken back to the glass-fronted prison where I had marked my eighteenth birthday, just one month before.

NINE

Anna: The Business of Sex

Amsterdam is a small city, a pretty city, in many ways a cultured city, but its chief attraction for many of the millions of tourists who come here is easy and – theoretically – guilt-free access to safe, legal and paid-for sex with the women who work in the Red Light District. Women like Olivia and me.

We had a stake in this sector of the 'hospitality' industry; our bodies formed part of its stock-in-trade, but there was also a wider, more sanitised, culture of sex in Amsterdam that only served to perpetuate the suffering we endured.

More than five million tourists visit Amsterdam every year – the vast majority of them from outside Holland. While many come for the art museums and pretty scenery, a significant number are drawn by the open availability of commercialised sex. The Sex Museum attracts half a million of those tourists and they are led through static displays celebrating the history and evolution of human sexuality. Of course, there's nothing wrong with that, except that the exhibits paint a sanitised and misleading picture of the sex industry – and the same is true of a second stop on the tourist trail, Red Light Secrets. This venue, a few doors away from our windows on *Achterburgwal*, promotes itself as the world's first museum of prostitution and, for the price of a €10 ticket, promises 'an exciting and candid journey' into the lives of the city's sex workers; it also draws almost half a million visitors. There's a message here: sex in Amsterdam is an industry, and like industry the world over, it has a long, largely unnoticed chain of suppliers and adjunct traders to meet the demands of its customers. The difference is that this business is focused on – indeed, it entirely rests on – the sale of women's bodies.

Olivia and I had a unique window on the organisation of prostitution in the Red Light District and, within a few short weeks of beginning work there, I realised we were part of a substantial organisation, dedicated to maintaining the public image of a well-managed and legal sex trade, but which was, in reality, underpinned by a toxic stew of illicit cash, forced sex, hard drugs and violent crime.

Every industry – legal or otherwise – has its owners, its managers and its workers, and beyond them its ancillary traders, providers and suppliers. Women like us were not, of course, top of the food chain in the Red Light District ecosystem; rather, we were its most fundamental element, the ones whose pain and endurance made it function. And there were – there are – a lot of girls like us.

In any given 24-hour period, around 700 prostitutes work in the windows of De Wallen. I say 'around' because there's no truly accurate or official data to provide hard facts; after it legalised the sex trade, Holland decided it didn't need to count the women who entered it. In the government's eyes,

Olivia and I were no different from any other self-employed trader – a bartender or a baker, a builder or a plumber, for example – and so there was no reason to record exactly how many of us existed. Nor are there reliable statistics to show how many people pay for sex in the Red Light District.

Semi-official accounts, published by tourism companies, claim that the total number of customers is less than a quarter of a million per year; but even the most basic maths shows this to be a gross underestimate, since it averages out at each woman in the windows servicing little more than one client a day. I may have skipped a lot of school, but I know how to count – and I could very definitely add up the number of people paying to fuck me.

Those numbers – what might be called my productivity – had begun to rise; in my first few weeks in the windows I serviced around eight customers a night, but in the summer of 2003 this grew to least ten – and sometimes more – men paying to rent my body over my nine-hour shift. There was a reason for this increase, and it's one which reveals the truth about the ruthlessly organised nature of the trade.

Although we had signed contracts with the rental agency, neither Olivia nor I had a permanent window. Instead, we took our places behind the glass when other, more established prostitutes were not using their rooms, and on the understanding that we had no guarantee that these would be available. To use an analogy that you might recognise from your own lives in an office, we were essentially 'hot-desking'. That might not seem like any great hardship – in fact, it might appear to offer the potential for some respite from the toll taken on us – but the tension between Ricardo's demands that we make as much money as our bodies could bear and the uncertainty of knowing whether we would be able to do so added an extra, unwelcome layer of mental stress.

Behind this was the inescapable logic that there were more women wanting – or being forced – to rent rooms than the number of these spaces licensed by the city authorities. Demand for the windows exceeded supply, leading to competition and rivalry; this would inevitably be reflected in both the prices at which Red Light District prostitutes were offered for sale, and in an escalation of what we were required to do for the money.

Under Ricardo's constant prompting, we finally persuaded the rental agency, through our 'reliability', to lease us permanent windows. Our new rooms were also on *Achterburgwal*, in the heart of the most heavily frequented Red Light District streets; more importantly, they were next door to one of De Wallen's most popular sex-tourist attractions.

Theatre Casa Rosso is impossible – both literally and in tourist-speak – to miss. It is listed in every guidebook as Amsterdam's most famous live sex show, and its extensive two-storey frontage is adorned with a giant pink neon elephant. Inside, 180 seats are arranged in front of a basic stage; on this an endless parade of young women strip, perform perfunctory light S&M displays and, for the apparent entertainment of the audience, insert bananas or pens into their vaginas. The highlight – if that's the word – of the show is a silent, mechanical naked coupling by a male and female performer, in full view of the audience.

Put as starkly as this, the live sex 'experience' doesn't sound particularly thrilling. Yet *Casa Rosso* is always busy; the club takes regular group reservations – a minimum of ten people per booking – from bachelor and hen parties, groups of football supporters on weekend city-breaks and from commercial tourist agencies. This constant footfall translates into extra business – extra demand – for the women in the windows on either side. Either aroused or emboldened by what they've just seen, men – and some women – regularly go directly out of the theatre and knock on the neighbouring glass.

Olivia and I now had two of these highly profitable rooms, beside each other on the second floor of the building. Next to us, two other young women worked in identical cubicles, and as that summer wore on, we got to know them as much as the Red Light District allows. We never knew their names because in De Wallen no-one probes too deeply into anyone else's business – and, in any event, no woman working in the windows ever uses her real name. But they did tell us a little about how they, too, came to be working there and we found that we had much in common.

They were a little older than us, probably in their early thirties, and both were Dutch. Because of that, they – and we – were unusual; only a small proportion, probably less than twenty per cent, of the girls in the windows came from Holland. So, in between clients, we talked and bonded over our similar stories. Just like us, neither of our new neighbours had actually chosen to rent her body; each had been forced to do so by a pimp who used extreme violence to force them into prostitution. Just like us, each was now suffering from the physical wear and tear of selling their bodies day in, day out. Just like us, they had begun to lose any hope of ever escaping the glass prison in which they laboured.

The more we talked, the more I saw the truth: that Amsterdam's liberal, legal and supposedly risk-free commercial sex industry was no more than a fantasy – a fiction maintained to keep the profits rolling in for those at the top, on the backs – quite literally – of those at the bottom. One phenomenon, one word, above all summed this up: pimp.

Behind every scantily clad woman touting for business in the windows of De Wallen, there was a man. A man who put them there, kept them there and took a cut of their earnings, or – most often – the entire amount. These pimps were universal and inescapable; they drove around in expensive cars or sat in bars on the street corners, constantly monitoring the productivity of 'their' girls. In normal business terms, you might think of them as managers; the system's administrators who kept the whole enterprise ticking over. But since the commercial sex trade is not a normal business, more a dangerous and corrupted ecosystem, these men were actually sharks – predator and parasite combined – and there was nothing and no one higher than them in the food chain.

Holland does not like to call these men pimps. Instead, and in an attempt to describe how they most typically ensnare their victims, they are universally known as 'loverboys', because, just as Ricardo had done with us, their most common technique to ensnare a victim was to pose as her 'boyfriend', groom her and then, when it is too late for her to find a way out of the supposed 'relationship', use violence to force her into prostitution.

From our vantage point on the second floor of the *Achterburgwal* building, I watched the way these loverboy organisations functioned. On the lowest rung were lone operators like Ricardo, newcomers to the Red Light District who controlled two or three girls. They were the most vulnerable, and the most at risk of having their women taken from them by their bigger, more experienced competitors. This, I discovered, was one of the reasons why Ricardo had been so insistent that Olivia and I found a permanent place to work; constantly shuttling between rooms on a casual basis marked us out as novices without any real protection, and exposed him to the risk of a rival pimp stealing us for himself. It also explained the new tattoo which appeared on his neck – the word 'Deadly', spelled out in bold English letters; a warning, I assumed, to anyone thinking of challenging him.

The competition to own young girls like us was serious and unequivocally violent. The biggest loverboy organisations were run by Turkish and Yugoslavian men; there were several such gangs, each owning between 90 and 120 girls who, for the most part, they had smuggled illegally into Holland from the broken countries that used to be part of the Soviet Union and its satellites. That meant these organisations were international sex traffickers as well as Red Light District pimps.

Since the law which legalised prostitution had done so specifically to reduce sex trafficking, the ease with which these criminal gangs operated was hard to explain. So, too, was their very existence in Amsterdam; neither Turkey nor those former Yugoslavian states were members of the European Union, meaning these men had no legal right to work in Holland. And yet they operated in full view. They patrolled the Red Light District, their arm muscles bulked up with steroids, skins glowing from tanning salons, hair heavily gelled. They employed lower-ranking criminals as errand boys whose job was to watch and to see how many customers the girls were getting and to deliver food, drinks, condoms and paper towels; the larger groups even took on apprentices and trained them up in the techniques of pimping. Some introduced the refinement of branding their prostitutes with tattoos bearing the name of their owners as a way to prevent poaching by rivals. Yet no one, not the city authorities, the agencies which rented the rooms, nor even the police, seem to question how these foreign gangs were able to function so brazenly – and the same casual attitude was applied to their victims.

Those who weren't from the eastern edges of Europe had been shipped in from South America, Asia and Africa. None of these women had the right, even under our progressive laws, to sell their bodies in Holland, and since most could speak little or no Dutch – let alone read or comprehend the room-rental contracts – at first I couldn't understand how they had managed to acquire their windows.

As it turned out, there was really no mystery – it was all a matter of commerce. These women – hundreds of them – were trafficked to ports in Italy or Greece, then simply driven across European borders until they arrived in Amsterdam, where the loverboy gangs handed over large sums in cash – we never found out to whom – to procure the official paperwork which allowed them to rent rooms.

When we were working in the windows and talking to these women, uncovering their stories was not quick or easy. Aside from the language barrier, their pimps were determined to keep them isolated; they knew that friendships with outsiders would make it harder to control their girls. That was another early lesson I quickly learned in De Wallen: friendship was forbidden.

Psychological isolation, though, was only one weapon in these pimps' armoury; in the same way that Ricardo controlled us with his fists, knives and his gun, the major gangs used violence as a matter of routine. Their girls were brutally beaten with metal baseball bats for daring to step even fractionally out of line, and – just as Ricardo continued to fuck Olivia whenever the mood took him – the top men were notorious for raping the prostitutes they owned. Towards the end of my first year on *Achterburgwal*, one girl was murdered by her pimp after she became pregnant and tried to insist on keeping the baby. This was the brutal reality underpinning the theoretically safe, consensual business of legalised prostitution. This was the world in which Olivia and I were struggling to exist.

In one way, at least, we were slightly better off than many of the other women around us. Although we were well on the way to becoming full-blown alcoholics, after our previous bad experience we never used drugs as a way of suppressing our pain, and we had even stopped smoking weed. By contrast, the pimping gangs positively encouraged their girls to become dependent on drugs since this provided another means of control. None of these young women were ever allowed to step outside their windows during shifts, so they had to call their pimps to plead for the cocaine, heroin and hash to which they had become addicted.

This sad little tableau played out beside and in front of my window every night, and between servicing my clients I watched a steady and dismal procession of runners – the gangs' apprentice pimps – speeding along the street to deliver drugs to the shattered women behind the glass. I got to know their faces, recognise their swagger, understand the ebb and flow of the river of misery in which they – in which we all – either swam, floated or sank.

Drugs to meet any need, taste or addiction were openly traded throughout the Red Light District. More than 150 coffeeshops sold a cornucopia of marijuana, skunk and cannabis resin to tourists; under the same official policy of *gedoogbeleid,* or tolerance, which had legalised prostitution, serving weed as an accompaniment to an espresso was perfectly legal – and indeed extremely profitable. Almost a quarter of all tourists coming to Amsterdam visit the coffeeshops, consuming more than 100,000 kilograms of soft drugs every year.

Neither Olivia nor I had any real problem with this; our own history of smoking weed would have made it hypocritical for us to criticise anyone else for doing so. But, just as with the organized pimping gangs, no one ever seemed to ask where all the drugs were coming from; whilst possession of small quantities of marijuana was allowed, growing – much less importing – it was strictly illegal. Similarly, hard drugs were theoretically strictly outlawed, yet the stuff was sold on every street corner; so where had it come from – and who was distributing it?

I don't believe anyone ever asked. I certainly didn't – because when Ricardo told Olivia and I that he had stopped dealing coke, I realised that the trade in narcotics was run by people a great deal more dangerous than our own, newly tattooed 'Deadly' loverboy.

Amsterdam simply absorbed these drug dealers, these pimps and their trafficked, brutalised women into the ecosystem of the Red Light District; they were the necessary ancillary arms of a substantial economy, as essential and ineradicable to the sex industry's lengthy supply chain as the small cottage industry of freelance traders who sold skimpy garments – our required work 'uniforms' – to the girls behind the glass.

That this world was violent, cruel and illegal seemed not to matter. Although police officers and undercover detectives were assigned to De Wallen, the former strolling through the alleys in pairs or patrolling the canal-side cobbles on smart mountain bikes, I never saw them stop a drug deal – and not one ever made any serious effort to check whether I, Olivia or any of the hundreds of other women in the windows were willingly selling their bodies.

Instead, it was the pimps who ruled the streets. That they did so absolutely and without any official interference or attempts at control was evident from the freedom with which they stopped tourists and journalists from taking photos in the Red Light District, sometimes enforcing this strict prohibition by throwing their cameras into the canals.

In the end I came to understand the fundamental truth about the place where I worked. Drugs and sex, cheaply priced and freely available, meant tourists – and, since tourists meant municipal money, nothing could be allowed to get in the way of this market in human misery. Violence – whether meted out by organised gangs or small-time crooks like Ricardo – was, if ever acknowledged, simply part of the cost of doing business.

By the end of 2003, our first year in the shop window of the commercial prostitution industry, I calculated that between us Olivia and I had each survived almost 300 shifts; we had both worked six nights a week – Tuesdays, for some reason, were traditionally low on customers, so Ricardo generously allowed us this one evening off – spending more than 3,500 hours locked up in our glass prisons. We were not yet nineteen years old, and I taken around 2,000 men inside my beaten and bruised body; Olivia had serviced almost as many.

Any one of these men – or any normal person who observed us – would have seen that we were miserable and barely functioning as human beings. Any of the customers who looked into our eyes before they penetrated us should have understood that we truly didn't want to rent out our bodies. But they didn't look. They arrived, they undressed, they thrust and they left without a hint of concern. I could count on the fingers of one hand the number of clients who had even asked my name; fewer still bothered to ask if we were all right, or noticed the pain they were inflicting.

We were on display in one of the world's most popular tourist destinations, yet seemingly invisible to anyone with the power to help us. But through the alcohol on which we were increasingly dependent, and the robot-like state it induced, we saw one thing clearly. Save for each other, we were alone in a cruel and vicious world, with no prospect of release; if we were to survive at all, we needed – quickly – to find a way to cope. It was almost 2004: it was time to learn the tricks of our trade.

TEN

Olivia: Tricks

We once thought we knew about sex. We once thought we knew about men.

In the two years before we began work in the Red Light District, we had told ourselves, with the fragile bravado of terrified children, that we knew the worst of the world and could handle it. We were wrong.

It was not as if we had led sheltered lives back home in our village; if nothing else, Ricardo's continual abuse had taught us to grit our teeth through the beatings and the pain of rough penetration. I had endured the humiliation of contracting chlamydia and the loneliness of a termination. Anna had somehow found a way to cope with her enforced prostitution to Ricardo's Iranian customer.

But nothing prepared us – nothing *could* have prepared us – for that first year of working in the windows of De Wallen.

The first truth we learned about the legalised prostitution business in Amsterdam was that whilst, in theory, we were independent, liberated women choosing freely to barter our bodies for financial reward, in reality we were neither independent nor free. The fundamental rule of this legalised meat market – a rule enforced by violence – was that we could never say no.

No matter how tired we were, no matter how sore, it was our job to provide satisfaction to our clients, however extreme their tastes. They turned up at our windows night after night, secure in the knowledge that the money in their wallets entitled them to do whatever they wanted with us.

Could we really not have refused? After all, the taxi drivers who often brought these clients to our windows on *Achterburgwal* were permitted to turn down a fare if the passenger seemed too drunk, too high on drugs or too dangerous. It was, I suppose, possible; unlike many of the prostitutes trafficked into the city from Eastern Europe, Anna and I were not desperate for money to feed a hard drug habit, and there were some nights when Ricardo was not watching us from the safety of a corner bar, monitoring how many men we accommodated. Yet our fear of him was so great, and our belief in ourselves so small, that rather than turn away someone who knocked on our windows we learned ways to put them off.

The most common demand we faced was to have unprotected sex. Naïvely, this shocked me: I couldn't understand how anyone would risk contacting a sexual infection, but they did – repeatedly. I lost count of the number of customers who assumed I would either suck them, or let them fuck me, without a condom, and then when I made clear that this wasn't part of the deal, offered extra payment to make me change my mind. I came to see that the reason for this was the basic idea of legalised prostitution; inside our glass boxes we were sexual servants, always available, always required to appear willing to fulfil any fantasy.

And some of our competitors – usually the trafficked women working for the large pimping gangs – were forced by their owners to have unprotected sex. I knew this from the stories they shared with Anna and I, and from clients who told us they could – and did – get this service from our rivals. But even had I been tempted by the extra cash, the thought of having to take them without a condom on made me feel physically sick.

Yet week in, week out, these men turned up, demanding 'bareback' – as it was generally described – as if it was their right. My dilemma was how to turn them down without losing the business and thereby risking another beating from Ricardo. Unlike Anna, I had always confronted danger with anger and, as the months wore on, I found that the best form of defence was attack. So whenever a client suggested unprotected sex, I challenged them loudly by saying, 'Yes, of course I'll fuck you without a condom, but I have AIDS – is that okay?'.

The outburst always shocked them; they looked at me as if I was mad, which struck me as ironic given the reckless stupidity of what they had asked for, and then sheepishly agreed that whatever they paid to do to me would happen through a layer of insulating rubber.

These little performances were effective, but subtly, gradu-ally, they wormed themselves under my skin. I found it ever-harder to disguise my contempt for the men who paid to penetrate me and almost impossible to shake off the disgust I felt for myself. Even my nightly intake of booze – and I had begun to drink ever more heavily – couldn't suppress these feelings completely, and through its haze I sensed that the temper outbursts I pretended to have were becoming real; my mind had started to slip from its moorings.

It was the same for Anna, though it was the alarming number of elderly men who made clear that they fantasised about underage sex that pushed her towards breaking point. Although she was now nineteen, and despite the physical toll on her body of our line of work, she still looked terribly young and seemed to attract customers who wanted her to pretend she was a small child. Their undisguised paedophilia made Anna feel even more dirty and disgusted than she had previously believed possible.

Eventually she found the courage to refuse the worst of these clients. But throughout that first year she, like me, was constantly faced with men who felt they had the right to abuse us in any way they saw fit. That was – and remains – the raw truth about 'consent' in the legalised sex trade; simply by standing in the windows we were assumed to have agreed to these assaults on our bodies.

Who were these clients? That was the second truth we learned. There is a misconception – one that we vaguely once shared – that people who pay for sex conform to a few easily recognisable stereotypes: lonely middle-aged businessmen, seedy, dirty old men, or those whose physical handicaps or extreme ugliness have made it otherwise impossible to attract a non-commercial sexual partner.

Of course, there were men like that, and many of them knocked on our windows. But others were even more troubled and several were very obviously mentally ill. One of my customers was a war veteran who was so severely traumatised and confused that he simply he sat in a corner of the room for the duration of his fifteen-minute session, never touching me, seemingly lost in his own visceral memories. Another seemed to be haunted by some kind of ghostly apparition; he, too, never entered my body – I don't think he even had an erection – but simply gibbered manically in six different languages throughout the time he paid for.

Drugs, of course, played a part in this. We quickly became used to dealing with people who were very obviously high on one of the wide variety of illegal substances on sale in the Red Light District. These men tended to be aggressive and more demanding and we had to learn how to cope with their volatility, then stop it escalating out of control. But with other clients, the drugs they consumed actually worked in our favour.

Anna had a regular customer who paid once a month to snort cocaine in her room, and then have her accompany him to the *Casa Rosso* live sex show next door. Here he passively watched the male and female performers listlessly fuck each other on the circular bed in the middle of the stage; he never wanted any sexual contact for himself, only to sit beside Anna and observe as the performance unfolded.

One incident, from later in our time in the windows, encapsulated the relationship between drugs and prostitution. A wealthy Arab sheikh, surrounded by muscular security guards, stopped at my window; he gave me €100 and arranged for his chauffeur to take both Anna and I back to his suite at the Amstel Intercontinental – the most luxurious five-star hotel in the city. We were escorted up to his floor in a private lift and found ourselves in a linked network of lavishly furnished rooms, each the size of a large apartment. What followed was surreal.

The sheikh dismissed his bodyguards and showed us around. The door to his private safe hung open and we could see stack after stack of €500 banknotes, as well as a stash of white powder in little bags. He pulled some of the notes out of the safe and thrust them into our hands, then helped himself to the drugs. Throughout the evening he snorted so much cocaine that he couldn't get an erection and was completely unable to have sex; in the end he abandoned the attempt, dismissed us and we left, well paid, but marvelling at the stupidity of rich men.

For the most part, however, our customers were not glamorously extravagant playboys, nor were they drug users rendered impotent by the substances they ingested. Rather, they were – or at least they looked like – normal people. A surprising number were young; others were conventional business types and family men: middle-class fathers, brothers, uncles with wives and children waiting at home – and with jobs that evidently paid enough to fund their visits to our windows.

Strangely, perhaps, we never really thought much about the men who visited us. That would have required some basic level of interest in them or their lives, and we didn't – we could not – allow ourselves to engage with them on that emotional level. For our own sanity we had to disengage our minds from what these 'normal men' did to our bodies.

Yet from time to time, we did wonder what it was that led them to pay us for fifteen minutes of such impersonal rubber-insulated sex. Curiosity evidently played its part; many of our clients were tourists – English, Chinese and Italian were the most common nationalities – drawn to the Red Light District by its international marketing as the world's first and most famous legal prostitution zone. To them, I think, we were no more than another attraction laid on by the City of Amsterdam for their brief amusement; no different in their minds from seeing the priceless artworks on display at the *Rijksmuseum*, or strolling through the floating Flower Market. We were a holiday experience, something to tick off their bucket list. In short, they paid to penetrate us because we were there – and because they could.

Did they ever wonder about us? Did they ever think about who we were and how we had ended up in the windows? Probably not. They must have realised from our demeanour, our complete disinterest in anything but their money, that we weren't doing this for our own pleasure. In the minds of the clients we were simply living, breathing sex toys to be used and then disposed of.

As well as the tourists, there was a substantial and ever-replenishing pool of customers who came to our windows bringing fantasies which, though legal, very obviously could not be satisfied in their normal lives. Some men brought their wives or girlfriends and paid to watch us pleasure their women with vibrators. But others had tastes which were far darker, far more extreme, than anything we had ever known. Paradoxically, these were by far the easiest clients.

They were always men. They came with one goal – their fetish – and since that didn't require a suck or a fuck, we preferred them to the customers with more conventional tastes.

The easiest of all was a regular customer who was aroused by feet. He handed over piles of cash for the privilege of licking my toes and insteps. Another frequent caller at our windows had developed an obsession with a transsexual prostitute who worked in one of the windows nearby; this man's fantasy – and one which he regularly paid to act out – was to hire Anna to watch as he sucked the transwoman's penis. Although this frequently disgusted Anna to the point where she could no longer bear to be in the room and slipped outside to smoke a cigarette, the client was so wrapped up in satisfying his fetish that he rarely noticed her leave. He came back time and time again, often high on cocaine. Generally during these drug binges he paid to sit in Anna's room, masturbating himself to climax while she talked dirty.

Men like these were easy money, since satisfying them involved little or no physical effort – though the constant exposure to these fetishes was starting to take a noticeable psychological toll. But they were the most anodyne of our 'specialist' customers; beyond them were those whose tastes ran to degradation and severe pain.

One was a French-Moroccan man, who turned up covered in bruises and asked Anna to penetrate him anally with a strap-on dildo. A Dutch customer – another regular – paid to be scolded, strangled and repeatedly kicked in the balls. One of Anna's most constant clients – he turned up at our windows almost every weekend – hired her to stand on his genitals, grinding the spike of her stiletto heels into his penis until it bled on the tiled floor.

Another always brought with him a pair of rubber gloves. He undressed and lay down on the bed; Anna had to put on the gloves, then grip, twist and torture his nipples before stubbing out a lighted cigarette on his chest. His skin was so badly cracked and broken from previous sessions that blood seeped out copiously throughout; this explained the rubber gloves – a barrier to infection, we presumed – though we never figured out why he insisted on playing the same rap music track throughout each encounter.

Other even less sanitary bodily fluids regularly featured in our clients' fantasies. Both of us were frequently paid to urinate over the bodies and faces of men – never the other way round; we would never allow a client to do that to us. As gross as this may sound – and indeed it was – the women in neighbouring windows told us that they were frequently asked to defecate on clients.

I want to be clear. I'm not sharing these extreme encounters with the aim of shocking you, but rather to paint a truthful picture of what we experienced throughout that first year in the windows, and to show the reality of working as a prostitute in the legalised sex industry. But I hope that you are shocked, because only those who have become anaesthetised to the suffering of others can view with equanimity behaviour so far from the edges of normal human sexuality. I know this because by the end of 2003, Anna and I had become completely desensitised.

In the beginning we had been surprised by what our fetish customers asked for. We thought that paying for the inflic-tion of pain and degradation was a strange way to come by pleasure. But by that Christmas – and yes, we worked over the holiday period – this faded away, and it no longer crossed our mind to wonder about how they had developed their obses-sions. All that concerned us was that Ricardo had put us in the windows with instructions to serve and satisfy; and since accommodating the fetishists paid well (although we never got to keep any of the extra money), and didn't involve any form of penetration, we welcomed them as the easiest of our daily stream of clients.

There were, though, other signs that the work was putting us under a dangerous mental strain. The first was a realisation that although we could recall everything that had been done to us during our shifts – every demand made, every penetration granted – neither of us could recall a single client's face. If, at the end of our shifts, anyone had told either of us to make a photo-fit of any of the multiple customers we had serviced, we would have been able to give only the crudest and most basic descriptions.

Of course, no one ever asked, but the meaning of this partial amnesia was not lost on us; just as our clients saw us as dehumanised sex machines, to us they were faceless and unmemorable – nothing more than mobile wallets from whom to extract the maximum cash at the least possible cost. Soon this led us to adopt the worst tricks and deceptions of the prostitute's trade, and – the second indication of our mental deterioration – to do so without shame or any appropriate fear of the consequences.

Most of the men who knocked on our doors wanted exactly what we offered in the sales pitch Ricardo had taught us to recite: '€50, suck and fuck'. But as the months passed, we began to find creative ways to avoid having to deliver on our promise. As soon as we got the clients through the door and into the room, we changed the rules without, of course, telling them. So after giving them the briefest and most perfunctory oral sex we could get away with, we refused to allow them to have intercourse unless they paid a further €50. Of course the men argued, rightly saying that we had quoted a single price for both a suck *and* a fuck. We responded by insisting that, in their eagerness to rent our bodies, they had not listened properly or had misheard. Our hope was that this would put them off; that they would be so frustrated or annoyed that they would pull up their pants and walk out. And often this worked. But, unfortunately for us, some of the men were either so rich or – more probably – so driven by their lust that they simply opened their wallets again and paid the extra money.

And so we found other ways to avoid being penetrated. I learned from the older, more experienced women in other windows that there are ways a woman can give a man the false impression that he has entered her. Chiefly, this involved surreptitiously slipping a hand between my legs at the crucial moment, so that a customer fucked my tightly clenched fist. Anna quickly adopted the same technique.

This worked surprisingly often, though some of our clients were evidently too experienced in the ways of the window girls to fall for the deception. They accused us of cheating them and demanded their money back. But we refused, explaining that there were no refunds in the Red Light District, and that because we had already given them a blow job, our pimp would not allow us to hand back any of the cash; that – in his view – it was the same as giving a 'freebie', something strictly forbidden and generally enforced by very physical punishment.

The threat of violence was an ever-present undertow in the narrow lanes and canal-side streets of De Wallen; pimps ruled the area and their word was the law. But occasionally customers were either so angry, so high on drugs or so naïve about the possibility of a beating that they became aggressive themselves. We learned the techniques to physically push these angry, self-pitying men out of our rooms and then quickly lock the doors behind them. Even then, some would throw bricks and stones at our windows, yelling obscenities and smashing the glass – damage for which the rental agency fined us heavily.

Yes, our behaviour was dishonest, but I don't feel any pangs of guilt about this. We felt no more pity for the clients we cheated than a professional card shark would have for a foolish man wandering into an illegal gambling den and expecting an honest game of poker. The more men we serviced, the looser the ties to our old upbringing and childhood values became, and the further we drifted away from any semblance of morality or honesty. We cheated, we faked – and in time we began stealing.

There was a basic bathroom in the building where we rented our rooms, and if the customer seemed like a promising 'mark' – someone we could either con or rob – we insisted that he went there to take a shower before sex. Typically he would partially undress, leaving his jacket or trousers on the bed before walking down the little corridor.

While one of us kept a careful watch, the other would search his clothes, find his wallet and steal the cash inside it; when the man returned and he found he was unable to pay us the extra €50 we demanded for a fuck, we simply shrugged and feigned innocence. Oddly, this often worked – a measure, perhaps, of the pervasive air of menace which was never far below the surface of the Red Light District. But some men, made confident by the notional legality of the commercial sex trade, were unafraid to stand their ground; they argued, they complained and they threatened us with a beating.

Those who don't know the reality of life behind the windows may ask why we didn't hit the panic buttons, installed inside every licensed room by order of the city council. Leaving aside our own criminal behaviour, the answer was simple. Pressing our alarms merely set off a siren on the wall outside the building; this invariably attracted a large crowd of spectators – mostly tourists, who appeared to view the excitement as just another show, put on for their entertainment in the Red Light District. Certainly they did nothing more useful than stand and watch.

We could, in theory, have called the police. But in reality, there wasn't time – the violence erupted so fast that they could not possibly have arrived in time to help. Phone calls from prostitutes were routed to the central police station; a desk officer there asked for the window's location and then checked to see if there was a patrol team nearby and available to respond. This always took ten or fifteen minutes – by which time the aggressive client had generally disappeared into the night.

Nor was there any point in phoning Ricardo. Again, in theory, as our pimp he existed to protect us – that, after all, was the sole justification for him taking half of the money we earned. But since he regularly punched and kicked us himself, the prospect of us receiving a beating from a customer didn't remotely concern him; he knew that it wouldn't stop us working the next night and that we could cover up the bruises with make-up. And so we learned to handle the problem ourselves, thrusting the furious clients out of the door, often throwing their clothes out behind them.

Sometimes, however, the men we cheated or robbed felt confident enough to stand their ground and take their grievance to the police. We both became accustomed to patrol officers turning up at our windows, responding not to a threat to our safety, but to a customer's complaint either that he hadn't received the sexual services he had paid for, or that we had stolen the money from his wallet. In most cases there was little the man could do to prove his allegations, and the police generally walked away without bothering to investigate further. But once we made the mistake of picking the wrong victim.

We had gone through our usual routine of distracting his attention by sending him off for a shower and then taking the banknotes out of his wallet, but it turned out that this customer knew precisely how many euros, and in exactly what denominations, he had when he walked in through our door. He went to the police, insisting that they search our rooms; it didn't take long for a detective to discover the particular combination of €5 and €10 notes we had stolen. Because reports from previous victims of our scams were on file, we were both arrested and held in jail overnight. Fortunately for us the man chose not to take the matter to court and we were released without charge. But it was a sign of how far we had fallen, of the risks we were now routinely running; and, in retrospect, it should have been a warning that we were in deep psychological trouble.

But that's hindsight. Back then no one – not the rental agency, not the police, not our pimp and – of course – not our customers gave a damn. But we, too, were victims, forced against our will to rent our bodies. To them we were just prostitutes; young, yes, and terribly vulnerable. But that was hardly unique; De Wallen was full of girls like us. And like them, we had become desensitised, unable to recognise the danger we were in.

By April 2004, we had been in the Red Light District six days a week for a full year; prisoners on display in our glass-fronted boxes, our bodies available for whatever demands our customers chose to make of us. We had learned the tricks of our trade, and in our desperation to avoid the hurt and degradation of repeated daily penetration, we had earned a reputation for cheating and thieving. Our names were now recorded as accused criminals in the files of Amsterdam city police, while in the offices of the rental agency we were marked down as women who attracted violence and gave De Wallen a bad name.

ELEVEN

Anna: Mind Games

Our hiding place was dark and cramped. We had crawled under a bed, our bodies squeezed together, rigid with fear as we listened to the sound of our apartment being ripped apart; a window being smashed, a door kicked in. Olivia's face was pressed against mine, her eyes wide with fear. Neither of us spoke – we barely dared to breathe; silence, complete stillness and the divan above were our only hope of escaping detection.

Footsteps – heavy, loud and angry – then a shaft of light as the bedroom door was flung open. My field of vision was narrowed to a thin rectangle by the bedframe; through it I saw boots approaching. I clenched my eyes tightly shut and stopped breathing altogether. When I opened them the point of a knife was inches from my face, slashing at me; paralysed with fear, I watched as it was withdrawn; then, in what felt like slow motion, thrust back, again and again.

It was 2005. We were in our own home – our one safe refuge from the nightly degradation of working in the Red Light District – and someone was trying to kill us. How had we come to this?

The answer was, of course, Ricardo.

Towards the end of our first year in the windows, his girlfriend had finally thrown him out of the house he shared with her and their child. We presumed she had finally had enough of his behaviour, his unfaithfulness and his criminal lifestyle, although we never discovered whether she knew that he earned his living from pimping. Ricardo never volunteered any information about his private life, and we knew better than to ask; difficult questions usually resulted in very physical retribution.

The first we knew of his eviction was when he arrived at our flat and announced that from then on, he would be living with us. He moved his clothes into Olivia's bedroom and expected us to look after him in the same way as his girlfriend; sorting out his meals and his laundry was added to our daily workload. For good measure, he also re-claimed Olivia's body, something he had largely neglected in recent times. I didn't need her to tell me that this was not something she wanted; even if I hadn't recognised exactly how exhausted and sore she was from servicing so many men in each shift, her dull and lifeless eyes spoke volumes. Ricardo must have seen this too, and, since he was taking half of her earnings, he knew exactly how many men had fucked her by the time he satisfied himself inside her; very evidently he didn't care. And so, night after night I heard the sound of her being raped – for that was what it amounted to – through the walls of the apartment.

Or rather, apartments. Plural. Because over the course of a year, Ricardo moved us into four different flats in the village. Each time he told us there was a problem with the lease, that somehow they had been rented to us illegally. Whether or not that was true, the moves served him well because they added to the uncertainty and isolation we were already enduring. From one day to the next, we never knew whether we would be forced to pack up our possessions and start over again in a new home.

It's easy with hindsight to see that that this was part of a much bigger scheme to keep us under his control. One night we got home to find the apartment had been ransacked while we were at work. Furniture was smashed, our clothes were scattered over the floor and our few bits of jewellery, as well as a large amount of our cash, had been stolen. At the time we accepted that this was a genuine burglary, although we knew there could be no question of reporting it to the police. Only later did we come to believe that Ricardo had staged the whole thing; it was just another one of the mind games he played to keep us unsettled and under his thumb.

It worked. There was literally no part of our lives he did not control. He dictated our work schedule, managing everything from the time we had to set off for Amsterdam to the one night a week we were permitted not to stand in our windows. If we wanted – more accurately, if our bodies were so bruised and battered that we *needed* – to change that evening off, we had to ask his permission. Sometimes he agreed, other times – for no purpose we could discern – he refused.

He took half the money we earned, leaving us to pay the agency's room-rental fees, and to buy the condoms, disinfectant and rolls of kitchen towels we got through every shift. He even made Olivia buy him a car – registered in her name for reasons we did not then grasp – so that he could drive us to and from De Wallen.

His violence was a constant presence in our lives, though an unpredictable one as we never knew exactly what would provoke him – or when.

I was in bed one evening when, through the walls, I heard the sound of Olivia crying out in pain. I couldn't tell what he was doing, but later found out that Ricardo was tormenting her by burning her back and buttocks with a cigarette lighter. I listened, horrified, as she begged him, repeatedly, to stop – but he refused. Eventually she couldn't take the pain any more; she rolled over and pushed him away. Moments later, I heard the sound of a heavy glass plate being smashed over her head and Olivia screaming for me to come and help her.

I ran into the room and saw the floor was littered with shattered glass. Olivia's face was badly cut and blood was pouring from her ear; as I reached and went to hold her, she fainted and fell down on the floor.

I freaked out and screamed at Ricardo. 'Look what you've done! I'm going to call the police. And we have to get an ambulance: I'm going to phone the emergency services now.' But he wouldn't let me; he told me to shut up, calm down and look after Olivia. I sat with her head in my lap trying to stem the bleeding until, eventually, she came to. It was very obvious that she needed medical attention but although I begged Ricardo to let me call for help, he still refused. Finally, I became hysterical, ran out of the flat and phoned the emergency services from a call box on the street.

When the ambulance arrived, Olivia was still bleeding from a deep cut by her ear. It was clear from the wound and the broken glass on the floor that she had been attacked. But with Ricardo standing beside us, glowering and threatening, neither she nor I had the courage to tell the truth about what had happened; instead, we covered for our pimp, making up a ridiculous story that she had slipped in the shower and hit her head on the bathroom floor. I was certain that the paramedics didn't believe our claims, but they didn't challenge us; nor did they report the incident to the police. If he hadn't known it already, Ricardo was absolutely confident in his complete and utter control over us.

Although there was little rhyme or reason to his attacks, there was one thing which was guaranteed to provoke Ricardo's violence: his fear that someone would steal us from him. Whether he saw that threat coming from a rival pimp or from one of the occasional customers who managed to combine a willingness to pay us for sex with a hypocritical zeal to save us from prostitution – and you can take it from me that these self-anointed abusers-cum-rescuers are a depressing fact of life in the Red Light District – the slightest indication that either of us had talked to someone he didn't approve of was certain to infuriate Ricardo. Something we soon learned to our cost.

We were, as always, working our shifts when a famous American rap star strolled along *Achterburgwal* with his entourage of minders and hangers-on. He stopped at Olivia's window and she recognised him. She opened the glass door and they chatted for a few minutes before he asked for her phone number. Half an hour later he called, asking her to go back with him to his hotel. This man was – I should be clear – not suggesting a date, or a free-of-charge party. No, he was a customer – and a promising one at that; given his fame and wealth, he would pay a great deal more than €50 for a fifteen-minute suck and fuck. And of course Olivia agreed.

But going with him would mean leaving her window – and, more importantly, being out of Ricardo's sight. That, as it turned out, was far more important to him than his half share of the much higher than usual fees she would charge the rap star. He had evidently been watching from his corner-bar hangout, and turned up at Olivia's window while she was on the phone with the rapper. He pushed through the door, demanding to know who she was talking to, and then summoned me to tell him what I knew. When she refused, Ricardo grabbed Olivia, threw her on the bed and punched her so hard that her head flew back and hit the wall. Then, with a can of Red Bull in his fist for extra emphasis, he beat her thighs and torso black and blue. After which he turned his attentions to me; if nothing else, he was an equal-opportunity abuser. And then he walked out, without a word, leaving Olivia and I sobbing and clinging to each other. The planned rendezvous with the rap star was, inevitably, abandoned.

Which is how, later that same evening, we ended up hiding under the bed, convinced we were about to die.

It happened, ironically, after we found the strength to request help for the first time – from the police. The extreme nature of Ricardo's violence that night had scared us so much that we asked one of the uniformed officers patrolling De Wallen to walk with us from our windows to the taxi rank where we were to get a ride home. We didn't dare tell him the truth about Ricardo; we knew by then that the police would never stand up to any of the pimps, and that all a complaint would accomplish was another vicious beating. So we lied and said we were worried about a crazy customer who had been bothering us.

When we got close to home, we told the taxi driver to drop us off a hundred metres away from our building. We didn't know if Ricardo had got there before us, so we crept closer and hid in some nearby bushes, peering through the leaves to see if there was any sign of him. We crouched there, cold and afraid, for at least half an hour. When we were as sure as we could be that Ricardo wasn't home, we rushed inside the flat, and double-bolted the locks so that, even using his key, he would not be able to unlock them. Then we turned off all the lights and sat, silently, on the bed, terrified but grateful for the peace and quiet. It didn't last long.

He had called Olivia several times that evening but she had refused to answer her phone. That, of course, infuriated him and he kept calling, leaving messages ordering her to pick up. That persistence should have been a warning, and as the hours passed, I grew increasingly frightened because I realised that we would eventually have to see him again, and the angrier he was, the more pain it would mean for us.

Ricardo came home, and tried to get in with the key. When this didn't work, he rang the bell. Repeatedly. We sat immobile, frozen with fear, hoping – naïvely – that he would go away.

Our front door was a cheap construction of glass and wood and the sound of it being kicked in spurred us into action. I looked around frantically, hoping to find a place to hide, hauling Olivia onto the floor and dragging her under the bed.

We held our breath as I listened to the noise Ricardo made as he raged through the flat. I noticed that he had not turned on any lights; somehow this made the situation even more terrifying. He went into the kitchen; a drawer scraped open and I heard the metallic rattle of a knife being pulled out. And then his legs appeared in the doorway. I watched his boots march towards the bed until they completely filled my field of vision. A pause. Silence. And then an exhalation of breath and a creak from the frame as he sat down heavily on the bed above us.

Time passed: seconds, probably, but each felt like an hour. And then, with only the soft material of the mattress above us offering any sort of protection, the tip of a blade slashed at our faces. Once, twice, I honestly don't know how many times the knife lunged close to our faces, but we twisted and wriggled to avoid its vicious point.

I am sweating as I write this. My fingers are white, my body rigid with fear. But it is not – or at least, not just – just the mental images of a blade passing within millimetres of my face that is causing this panic. It is something far, far worse. It is the absence – the total and irreversible absence – of any memory of what happened next which terrifies me now. Both I and Olivia have tried to recall what took place immediately after Ricardo attempted to stab us, but we cannot. The last thing we can remember is hugging each other, numbed and shaking under the bed. At some point Ricardo must have left the flat, but we have no memory of him doing so. We have worked with counsellors, doctors and psychiatrists; we have been given the most advanced psychological help available – yet nothing we do works.

I have been told that this, in itself, is a sign that what Ricardo did to us was so brutal that our minds were unable to process it and have made their own independent decisions to lock the memory away as the only way to protect our sanity. I know this was meant to comfort me – to reassure Olivia and I that our brains will stop us from re-experiencing this trauma. It doesn't – in fact it makes it worse. Because I can remember almost everything else that Ricardo did to Olivia and I – the extreme violence, the horrific abuse and the complete degradation he inflicted on us. But I know that beyond this he did something so terrible, so much worse, that we have to be protected from the memory of it. And that is utterly terrifying.

Ricardo learned something from our response to the attack. He saw that neither the frequency nor the viciousness of his assaults was able to drive a wedge between me and Olivia; if anything, they had the opposite effect, binding us closer together than ever. He must have realised that this posed a potential problem, since it might, at some point in the future, give us the strength to resist him properly. And so he began an insidious campaign to divide us.

Throughout the five years we had known him, Ricardo had never shown the slightest interest in me sexually; although he seemed eager to fuck as many women as he could – in addition to his girlfriend and Olivia – and despite his extensive appetite for pleasure, he had never even flirted with me, let alone tried to get me into bed. Now, that changed.

One evening Olivia and I had small argument. It was nothing more than a minor squabble over something completely trivial, but it left me upset and uneasy. Around halfway through my shift, Ricardo turned up at my window and asked to come inside. This was unusual – he very rarely stepped across the threshold of our working rooms – and I sensed immediately that something was wrong. He pulled the curtain closed after him, hiding us from sight and then lunged at me, groping my half-naked body and trying to kiss me on the mouth.

I was taken completely by surprise, but I managed to break free and push him away. Then, without a word, he turned round and walked out. I was already exhausted from servicing a succession of clients, and I had recently stopped numbing my pain with drink, so the incident tipped me over the edge. I was shaking uncontrollably and knew that I couldn't work any more that night; instead, I got dressed and walked out. I didn't even stop to tell Olivia I was leaving.

In between customers, over the next few hours Olivia tried to ring me; since we normally spoke several times every night, when I didn't answer my phone she began to panic. She phoned Ricardo, asking if he knew where I was and why I wouldn't talk to her; he feigned ignorance, telling her he hadn't seen me since the start of our shifts. Her calls to my phone grew more frequent and her messages, begging me to pick up, more urgent. Finally, I answered and told her what had happened. She was as shocked and confused as me, but we decided that when Ricardo brought her back to the flat, we would confront him together.

For the first time he was faced with the two of us, angry, united and demanding an explanation, but cunning as always, he saw this as an opportunity to create conflict between Olivia and I. He didn't deny touching me, but insisted that he was only trying to offer some comfort because he knew that we had argued. And he complained that I was crazy, that I had lost my already-tenuous grip on reality.

It was a clever and manipulative performance, and although both Olivia and I made it clear we knew he was lying, in some subtle way the damage was done. By sowing a tiny seed of doubt in Olivia's mind – that I had welcomed his advances and that I was lying to her about it – he had found a way to force a crack in our love for each other. Divide and rule were the names of his mind games – and they were working.

From never having a cross word, Olivia and I began to argue. Mostly it was petty quarrels, the sort of silly and short-lived arguments that flare between any two young flatmates, but twice in quick succession these escalated into nasty and bad-tempered extended fights. The worst of these happened one afternoon before our shifts, in the living room of the flat. I can't remember how it started, but I'm sure Ricardo provoked it, and he looked on in delight as Olivia and I actually came to blows; after watching us grapple for a few minutes he stepped in, laughing out loud, and separated us. I stormed off to my bedroom, smashed a glass and used the shards to cut myself. The pain of doing this brought me to my senses and I quickly covered the marks with make-up, determined that Olivia should not see what I'd done. But later that night, in a break between customers, she found me and was appalled; she hugged and held me close and we apologised to each other. And then we cried until neither of us had any tears left.

The cutting was a sign of how seriously disturbed I was becoming and in the end I decided I had to get away – from Ricardo, from the flat and, for the first time in almost a decade, from Olivia.

I had not seen, and had barely spoken to, my father since starting work in the Red Light District. He had made plain his disgust at what I was doing and had effectively cut me out of his life. I can't say I entirely blame him – though I did wonder if his attitude towards me could have been less judgmental since he should have realised that I was being forced to prostitute myself in the windows.

His partner – the girlfriend for whom he had abandoned my mother and I – owned a house in Amsterdam that she rented out to supplement their income and it happened to be empty. They were happy to let me lease it – at full market price – so I once again packed up my few belongings, took a taxi into the city and, for the first time in my life, found myself alone.

In other circumstances, the change might have been the spur I needed to rethink my life, and break free from Ricardo and from the commercial sex trade. Perhaps if I had not been so damaged, or if my family had felt able to intervene, I would have taken a long, hard look at myself and realised that I was sinking, slowly but inexorably, in a cold and dangerous sea. But I couldn't. I just didn't have the strength – mental or physical – for that fight.

And so, without missing even one shift, I carried on opening my mouth and spreading my legs for the constant stream of men who turned up at my window. And even though I was out of his immediate control, I carried on handing over half the money they paid to Ricardo; I honestly don't think it occurred to me that I could refuse. In fact, the only differences in my working situation were geographical – the agency moved me to a different room in *Stoofsteeg*, a little alley across the street from Olivia's window on *Achterburgwal* – and the fact that I now had to cope without the comfort of her presence next to me.

Although we were no longer in the same building and our close friendship had been somewhat fractured, De Wallen is so small and the sex-work community so interwoven that we still saw each other before and after our shifts. Those meetings were terribly painful; we had always been so close, through good times and bad, and I think we both knew deep down that the love we felt for each other still burned, that it was simply buried beneath the mental walls I had tried to erect. Even though they were now disintegrating, I continued to hide behind the rubble, keeping myself out of Olivia's reach.

There was one sign that our connection was – just – still alive. Every day, one of us still made enough sandwiches for us both, and brought them to work to share, should we get the chance of a moment together. It was a small and terribly weak flicker of hope, but it was there and faintly visible. And thank God it was.

Very soon after moving into my new house, I had begun to drink again. I was depressed, traumatised and now alone, and I didn't have any fight left in me. So I turned back to the bottle, anaesthetising myself with alcohol, following its deceptive course down the road to ultimate self-destruction After each gruelling day of 'work', I drank from the moment I fell through the door of my empty house, waiting for the welcome loss of consciousness which the booze eventually induced.

I woke, bleary and hungover, at around four in the afternoon, and mechanically prepared snacks and yet more drink for the night ahead before setting off for my window. My entire existence had shrunk to three basic functions: drink, get fucked, sleep. Repeat six nights a week, four weeks every month, twelve months per year. Looking back now, it is clear that my mind was coming apart at the seams, and this led me to cross one of the indelible red lines of the Red Light District – and, by doing so, to put myself at very real physical risk.

It was – and it remains – a fundamental rule of working in the windows never to mix business with pleasure. I learned to see the men who knocked on my glass as nothing more than mobile wallets; creatures to be emptied of both semen and cash in the quickest, least painful way possible. Fraternising with them was absolutely forbidden; they couldn't pay to fuck me and simultaneously be my friend. That was the law of the urban jungle in which I earned my living – and it was strictly observed by every woman selling her body there.

I can't remember exactly when – much less why – I first broke this commandment, but by the end of 2005 I had fallen into a very dangerous pattern. If a client came to my window who showed some spark of humanity – someone I felt I could speak to and maybe even laugh with – I invited them to come back later and hang out with me when I finished work.

It wasn't a question of sex – I never let any of them touch me outside business hours. I was lonely and longed for some kind of normal human connection. That was bad enough, but I was so desperate for some kind of friendship that I started taking them back to my house, drinking and partying until I collapsed from exhaustion or drink. It was reckless and terribly dangerous – I didn't really know anything about these men and any one of them could have raped or even killed me; God knows there was never any shortage of men with violence on their minds loitering in the dark alleys of the Red Light District.

Fortunately for me, Olivia found out about these sessions and immediately put a stop to them. She hadn't known that I was drinking again – let alone so heavily and in such risky circumstances – until a man she didn't know knocked on her window and asked if she knew where I was. Since we never gave our names to customers, she was instantly suspicious and demanded to know how he knew mine. He told her that he had spent the previous night with me, not as a client, but drinking and partying at my house. She was – quite rightly – absolutely furious. She told the man to fuck off, closed her curtain and phoned me.

Memory is a strange thing. Although there are large parts of my life I cannot recall, I remember exactly what she said to me when I picked up. 'Are you fucking stupid? Why are you taking clients to your home?' I could hear the anger in her voice, but I could also sense that it was borne of worry, not hatred; her love, her tenderness pierced the booze clouding my brain and I starting crying. I said, 'Do you think I want to do this? The truth is that I'm an alcoholic; I drink every night until I collapse at seven in the morning.'

Olivia begged me to go back to the apartment. She said she needed me and that she couldn't go on working alone. I realised that I had longed to hear her say those words and that it was being apart from her that had led me to start drinking again. And I understood then, beyond any doubt, that our friendship – our love for each other – still burned bright. Reluctantly, I agreed to think about it; I understood that I needed Olivia's love and support, but I also knew that Ricardo remained a substantial barrier between us, and that for as long as he lived with her in the flat, neither of us would be safe.

Which is when – for the only time since he had latched on to us five years earlier – I heard Olivia say that she wanted to find a way to be rid of him. This was progress, the first indication that his power over us both – once so complete – might be weakening.

I vowed never again to invite clients back to the house and soon I stopped drinking altogether. I can't say I recovered my health fully – I'm sure I no longer resembled the childlike waif who had proved so attractive to my paedophilic customers – but I knew Olivia and I were getting back to our old relationship. We started eating meals together – proper meals, not the soup and sandwiches upon which I had existed for the past year – which Olivia cooked and brought over to my house after our shifts ended.

But Ricardo remained a problem. He continued to turn up at our windows at the end of each night, counting up our earnings and taking half for himself. Neither of us could think of a way to stop him without risking a vicious beating; we knew, too, that given his attempt to stab us, and his earlier threats to put a bullet in our heads, punches might be the least of our problems if we tried to escape from his clutches. The same problem applied to kicking him out of the flat; and so, for the time being, we continued to live our lives on the constant knife-edge of his violence.

It would be another gruelling six months of being a prisoner inside our glass jails before we finally found the courage to free ourselves from him.

TWELVE

Olivia: Normal

For the second time in as many years I was pregnant. For the second time I faced up to a flurry of conflicting emotions: shame, humiliation, regret and fear. As before, the rational side of my brain told me that keeping the baby was out of the question – and, to be brutally honest, given the identity of man who had put it there, I had no real desire to do so – but reason and emotion are two very different creatures. Termination was the sensible and responsible option – not that I had any real choice – but there is always a psychological cost to be paid, and although I pushed my feelings to the back of my mind, I dreaded the prospect of returning once again to the clinic.

The only slight positive was that this time Anna would be coming with me. Although we were still living separately, seeing each other only at work in breaks between customers, the fact that she insisted on being at my side was a sign that our fractured relationship was beginning to mend. It was the only shaft of light on an otherwise miserable day. This time the procedure was much more painful; for reasons I can't recall – if anyone explained them, I was in no fit state to understand – it was carried out under local anaesthetic. When it was over and the doctors sent me home, I was bleeding profusely and in agony.

The man who had caused this, was, of course, Ricardo. His demands for sex had diminished slightly – an indication, if I had ever thought about it, that he was taking his pleasures elsewhere – but his refusal to use protection was absolute and unquestionable. He was the only man who penetrated me without a condom; he was the only possible sperm provider – I couldn't bring myself to think of him as the father of this unwanted child, since that word implied a connection I no longer felt with him.

Nor did he feel anything for me. When I told him, which I had to do as the termination would interrupt the flow of money I was making for him, his response was just as indifferent as it had been the first time. Get it out, get over it, get back to work. No questions, no sympathy, no interest other than how soon I could be back in my window.

I think, though, that he had begun to realise that his grip on me was beginning to slip. Despite the frequent beatings – and they never stopped – he sensed that his best efforts to sever the bond between Anna and I had failed, and that we might, in time, break free of him. That, certainly, would explain his reaction when I made the mistake of disrespecting the leaders of one of the Turkish pimping gangs with whom he competed for business.

It happened one hot evening in the spring of 2006. I was standing in my window, the door half-open to let in some cool air and get rid of the stink of sex and sweat, when four of them passed by. I knew these men; I knew the violence with which they terrorised the women they trafficked to work for them and I knew not to cross them or even attract their attention. But that night – whether from exhaustion, stress or because I was losing my instincts for self-preservation – I couldn't help myself. I dared not just to make eye contact, but to laugh at them.

Male ego is a fragile thing. I knew that much from the thousands of men who had paid to fuck me, as well as from absorbing the lessons Ricardo taught me with his fists. Yet as I watched the arrogant, swaggering group of pimps passing by, I saw that their jeans, tightly stretched over the crotch to emphasise their manhood, were tucked at the bottom into half-length Ugg boots. This was how Dutch women dressed and it made the gangsters look ridiculously effeminate. And so I burst out laughing. The Turks looked at me as if I were road kill – and in their mind that's probably what they saw in my future. I knew then that I had crossed a very dangerous line.

Within half an hour Ricardo appeared at my window. As usual he had been drinking in a nearby bar, which is where the gang of Turks had found him. Now they were lined up a few metres behind him, and their body language no longer struck me as funny; they were cold, determined and angry, and had, very clearly, ordered my pimp – my supposed protector – to bring his bitch back into line.

He didn't waste words. 'You are going to apologise to these guys because you laughed at them. Do it. Do it now.' Normally, I would have nodded my head and done as instructed, but that night something snapped. I'd had enough and from somewhere summoned the courage to stand my ground. I told him I wasn't going to apologise to the Turks – and, anyway, how did they know I hadn't been laughing at something, or someone, else?

Ricardo's reaction was swift, brutal and entirely unexpected. Although I was well used to his willingness to use violence, he had always done so in private; he had never let anyone other than Anna see him hit me. This time was different. Perhaps because he didn't want to lose face in front of his rival pimps, perhaps because he sensed that his control over me was eroding, he grabbed my face, twisting and pinching the skin until he forced me to say sorry to the Turks. Even then I tried to retain some shred of dignity, loading my voice with sarcasm and insincerity as I offered the required apology. Evidently they were not sufficiently fluent in Dutch to spot this, and swaggered off, 'honour' satisfied. Ricardo gave my face one last squeeze and told me to get back to work; he then stalked off, back to the bar and his shots of Hennessy.

Though he couldn't have known – if he had, I would already have received a beating – the first fragile seeds of resistance had been planted a few weeks earlier. I had been standing behind the glass, waiting for clients, when a boy I had known years before spotted me. I hadn't seen him for three years and he was surprised to find me working in the windows. He stopped and, for a few innocent minutes, we chatted like old friends. Nothing sexual happened; he didn't ask to come inside or offer to pay for me for sex, and for the first time since I had been forced into prostitution, I had a hint of how real people interacted with each other. Boy meets girl and – unlike the rules of life in the Red Light District – does so on equal terms.

The boy's name was Roger. He wrote his mobile number down on a scrap of paper and said that I should call him if I ever wanted to talk or go out for a quiet, friendly drink. I snatched at the note, looking round to check that Ricardo wasn't lurking around to see; then I went inside and hid it at the bottom of my bag.

I wonder now if I truly realised what I was doing. I certainly knew that if Ricardo found the piece of paper, he would beat me black and blue. I knew that it was far too dangerous to keep it, and that it would eventually be discovered. And yet I could not bring myself to throw it away; it represented the first tiny hint of normality, the first slender hope of a regular life. And so I buried it underneath my make-up and cigarettes, and prayed that it would go undetected.

It might well have done so, had it not been for a seller of pirate CDs. He was an immigrant – probably an illegal one – from somewhere in Africa, one of the loose and floating community of 'independent traders' who hawked dodgy goods on the streets of De Wallen; one evening, several weeks after my brush with the Turkish pimps, he knocked on my window. It was a slow night and so I let him in and quickly flicked through his collection of discs. He was in my room for no more than five or ten minutes – and he never laid a finger on me – so it was just bad luck, or bad timing, that Ricardo saw him leave.

For reasons I never understood, Ricardo had a peculiar paranoia about other dark-skinned men having sex with me. Whether this stemmed from some deep personal insecurity or was just another of the mind games he played to keep me unsettled, he had repeatedly told me to refuse customers whose colour matched his own. He had never actually done anything to enforce this prohibition, and was perfectly happy to collect his half-share of my earnings every night without any questions asked, but the sight of the CD seller emerging from my room enraged him. He jumped to the completely false conclusion that I had given the man a 'freebie', or perhaps traded a blow job for a couple of the discs – a cardinal sin in the rules of our business.

For the previous few weeks, Ricardo had started to pick me up early from my shifts; he would arrive at 2 a.m., count out the cash and tell me to gather up my belongings. Then, leaving Anna still working, he drove me back to the flat. So when he turned up that night I didn't immediately realise anything was wrong. We walked to the car and set off back towards our village as usual. But a few minutes later I saw that we weren't taking the normal route. I asked Ricardo where we were going; he didn't reply. As we sped, in silence, through empty streets towards the outskirts of Amsterdam, I felt increasingly afraid – and then I remembered that the paper with Roger's phone number was lying at the bottom of my bag.

Ricardo turned off into a deserted industrial estate. It was dark, eerily quiet and completely isolated, and he parked in front of an empty building; then he demanded I hand over my bag so he could search it. I knew I dare not let him see the note and angrily refused. He got out of the car, strode round to my side and pulled the door open; he pushed me down in the seat, using his body to stop me struggling and put his hands round my throat. He began to strangle me, hissing that unless I handed over the bag and let him search it, I would die just like Mary, who had been murdered by her boyfriend.

I cannot tell you how long this lasted. Realistically it must have been no more than a minute or so, but it seemed to me to be happening in slow motion and every second felt like an hour; I only knew that I was losing consciousness and that my vision was going dark when the beam of a torch flashed through the window and I felt the grip on my windpipe loosen. As my sight returned, I saw a uniformed policeman standing beside the car, pulling Ricardo off me. I crawled out onto the rough ground and screamed at the officer, 'He's trying to kill me – please, please stop him.' The cop arrested Ricardo on the spot, wrenching his arms behind his back and snapping handcuffs over his wrists. Then he drove us to the nearest police station, locked Ricardo up in a cell and began questioning me.

While I was waiting at the station, Anna called my phone and when I tearfully told her what had happened, she locked up her room and rushed down to the station in a taxi. Although the attack was traumatic and distressing, Anna and I had at least realised that the deep emotional bond between us had fully mended.

Towards dawn, the police told us Ricardo would be held in the cells overnight and said we should go home. I couldn't face returning to the flat in the village, so we went back to Anna's house in Amsterdam. We were both tired beyond anything we had known before, but neither of us could sleep; instead we sat together, talking about what had happened, and telling each other that my brush with death could turn out to be for the best. Surely, we reasoned, Ricardo would be charged with attempted murder – and that meant we would be free of him.

The police phoned me later that morning. I was ordered to go back to the station to make a full statement; Anna and I looked at each other, our hopes rising. We hoped too soon.

When I got to the station I was met by a detective who, like Ricardo, was from Suriname. He led me into an interview room and I was shocked to see the man who had tried to kill me lounging comfortably in a chair beside a desk; he looked as though he hadn't a care in the world. He didn't.

The detective began chatting casually with Ricardo in a language I didn't understand. It took a few minutes before it dawned on me that, although Dutch is the official Surinamese language, what they were speaking was the Creole-based patois used by ordinary people on the streets there. I only recognised it because I had heard Ricardo slip into this dialect a few times. Then, to my horror, the cop and my pimp began to laugh and joke together.

When it came to my turn to talk – to tell my side of the story – I found it hard to speak. I knew beyond any doubt that Ricardo had spun some bogus tale to the detective, and that although he fully understood that I was being pimped by the laughing man opposite me, he had decided to believe him. I tried, God knows I tried, to plead for help. I said Ricardo forced me to work in the windows; I told the cop about the beatings and the mental torment he put both Anna and I through. The man just shrugged; he said that unless my pimp was caught in the act of making me rent my body, as the law stood there was nothing the police could do.

Somehow, the fact that he had been arrested with his hands round my throat was ignored. As a known prostitute – and one whose tricks and thefts from clients had previously brought me to police attention – I was to be disbelieved and disregarded.

An hour later, Ricardo walked out of the station, pulling me along behind him. He had been released without charge, and I had been returned to him as if I were nothing more than a piece of lost property to be reunited with its owner. All the hope and dreams of freedom that Anna and I had allowed ourselves to reach for just a few hours earlier had evaporated. And, as disbelief gave way to anger, I knew that the police would never help us escape from sexual slavery. We went back to the flat and he beat me to a pulp. When Anna arrived a little while later, she found me sprawled on the floor, exhausted, bruised and clearing globs of blood from my mouth and face; as she knelt down to help me, Ricardo punched and kicked her as well.

We knew then that there was no one in the official world we could rely on for help. All we had was each other, and it was up to us, and us alone, to find a way of getting out of Ricardo's control. And we realised that if we were to do so, we needed to get protection.

In the Red Light District – a place, should I need to remind you, that is theoretically safe and well regulated – there are two major types of criminal organisation: the pimping gangs and the drug dealers. Our three years in De Wallen had taught us that the two groups operated independently and, at least in relative terms, without too much tension. In essence, whilst they were each the alpha predators of our polluted seas, since both fed on the desires or stupidity of the millions of tourists who came to get laid or get high (or both), their businesses had a symbiotic and complementary relationship. The pimps didn't deal drugs, but bought from the dealers what they needed to keep their women docile; similarly, the dealers didn't trade in women, but provided the cocaine and weed which the men who paid to fuck us often demanded.

We had got to know some of the dealers and – however strange this might sound, given their line of work – found them generally to be pleasant enough. Occasionally, if I had a customer who asked if I could get him some drugs, I negotiated a good price with the dealers, and took a percentage of the cash for myself.

I'm not proud of this but drugs and sex were the lifeblood of the Red Light District, the industrialisation of 'pleasure' on which it ran, and to survive there I had to conform. That was the fundamental lesson drummed into us, night in, night out, over three years. And we learned not just to abandon any hold on conventional morality, but also to find an accommodation with this loss.

We learned one other thing. If Ricardo knew he had to show respect to the bigger pimping gangs, he feared – absolutely and with good reason – the major drug dealers. Anna and I had got to know one of these men fairly well; his name was Elijah, he was a major cocaine supplier, in his mid-thirties and – by chance – also from Suriname. From our first nights in the windows, he stopped to chat with us. We grew to look forward to his visits – always brief and never sexual – because he lightened the misery of our shifts with jokes and laughter. Most crucially, though, he also talked to Ricardo, making it clear that in some unspoken way we were under his protection.

This, then, was the man on whom we pinned our hopes after the police turned me away that morning in May 2006.

But if our tentative alliance with the District's most powerful coke dealer offered some defence while we worked, my most immediate problem continued to share my bed and to demand sex as and when he felt the need. I knew that I could no longer cope with Ricardo alone, so I begged Anna to come home. She wasn't – yet – ready to do so, but I could feel that in time we would be reunited, and that when we were, the two of us could join forces against our abuser.

In view of the hell we had gone through since Ricardo first latched onto us, it was ironic, then, that the spur for our escape from Ricardo was a foreign holiday.

One night after work, Ricardo announced that he wanted to go back to see his friends and family in Suriname. We, of course, had provided the cash to make this possible – by this time we had handed over hundreds of thousands of euros to him – and Anna and I were required to buy plane tickets to accompany him.

Please don't misunderstand this 'invitation'; it had nothing to do with sentiment or Ricardo wanting us to go on holiday with him. Instead it was an acknowledgement that he was worried about losing us and the income stream that we provided. So little did he care whether we wanted to go that he might as well have stuck us in the aircraft hold.

In other circumstances we might have welcomed the trip; we were worn out after three years of continuously renting our bodies and any respite was welcome. But neither Anna nor I wanted to go to Suriname, and we most certainly didn't want to spend time with Ricardo. The financial cost, too, was high; in addition to our air fares, we had to pay the room agency two weeks' advance rent for our windows, knowing that even if it sub-let them to other women while we were away, we would be very unlikely to get the money back.

You might wonder why we agreed to go with Ricardo; why did we not simply tell him to go on his own. There is an answer – though we did not know it at the time – and it has a name: Stockholm syndrome.

This condition, first documented thirty years before we met Ricardo, causes prisoners to develop a psychological dependency on their captors – they experience trust and affection instead of fear and hostility, which is what an outsider would understandably expect victims to feel. In hindsight, we can see that this is what we were suffering from during those years, and without the mental space and clarity to recognise our situation for what it truly was – one of entrapment, powerlessness and abuse – we were simply unable to break free. Ricardo may never have held us behind locked doors, but in every mental sense he was our jailor – and we were very definitely his prisoners.

The trip was as miserable as we had feared. Suriname is a small, impoverished state, next door to Brazil on the Atlantic coast of South America. As a tropical country it is hot and wet all year round and the house Ricardo rented from his family was filthy and overrun with insects and lizards; to make matters worse, there was no hot water to wash in. Ricardo largely ignored us throughout the fortnight we stayed there – confirmation, if we needed it, that our presence was no more than a way of him stopping rival pimps in De Wallen from recruiting us. He left us alone in the squalor of the property while he drank and partied with his friends and family. But if he rarely bothered to speak to us, he was happy to let his fists do the talking, frequently punching my face and body for some perceived slight or insubordination.

The holiday did, though, have one positive outcome. At the end of June, after a fortnight in Suriname, we managed to persuade him that he was losing too much money by keeping us away from work, and he reluctantly sent us back to Amsterdam alone.

Although we had to go straight back to work, the next two weeks were the happiest times we had enjoyed since meeting Ricardo. For the first time in five years we were free of his constant supervision, his demands for money and – in my case – sex. We spent our non-working hours at Anna's house, sleeping, laughing and rediscovering the bonds of love which had become frayed; these precious, carefree days were our real holiday that year.

One night, shortly before Ricardo was due to return, I made a decision. I told Anna that I was tired of being his punchbag, fed up of giving him half the money my body earned; I said that I could not – would not – go back to live with him. There and then we agreed that as soon as possible, I would move in with her.

Where did this courage come from? How did I find the strength to shake off the Stockholm syndrome that had ruled my life for so long? It was another glimpse of normality that had made the difference.

I had stayed in touch with Roger, the young guy from my past. Although he had been shocked that night to discover I was working as a prostitute, he hadn't judged or rejected me because of it. We texted and phoned back and forth until one Tuesday evening in early July – my night off from the windows and while Ricardo was still away – we arranged to meet up.

It had been a glorious summer's day, and the air was still warm as Anna and I arrived at the *Twiske*, one of Amsterdam's most popular nature parks. Happy families and courting couples shared barbecues or swam in the clear waters of the river that runs through it. Roger was waiting for us with a friend of his, and the four of us spent the evening relaxing on the sand, laughing and drinking. The hours flew by in a blur of happiness and under cover of darkness, Roger and I slipped away and made love on a stretch of deserted beach. I was astonished to find myself wanting him and enjoying the sex; there was no aggression, no fear, just mutual attraction and respect. In that moment I discovered what had been missing from my experience with Ricardo: the attention of a man my own age who was gentle, honest and caring. And if the sand left dull, red scratches on our naked bodies, we laughed and relished them as the signs of our tenderness.

It was 3 a.m. before I thought to check my phone. Ricardo had come back from Suriname a few days earlier and I had been avoiding him as much as possible; now, when I looked at the screen I saw there were several missed calls and a message. I called up voicemail and heard his voice, crackling with anger: 'Where are you? I know you're off having fun somewhere. Answer your fucking phone.'

His arrogance sealed my decision. I wasn't going back to Ricardo – hell, I wasn't even going to phone the bastard. I was ashamed of allowing him to turn me into a prostitute – of the chlamydia he had given me, the pregnancies and terminations he had caused and the violence he had inflicted on me and on Anna. That evening on the little beach had shown me a glimpse of what normal life looked like, and I wanted more of it. If I couldn't – yet – see a way to get away from the Red Light District, I was determined that we would escape from the pimp who lived off the money our bodies earned there. Towards dawn, I kissed Roger a temporary farewell, promising that this night would not be the last we spent together, and then Anna and I went back to her house, tired but for the first time we could remember, happy. We locked the doors and fell into bed.

We were woken at 6:30 a.m. by the sound of Ricardo pounding on the front door with his fists, yelling at us to open up and let him in. As we huddled together under the blankets, we both had flashbacks to the night when we hid from him under a bed and he stabbed at us with the kitchen knife. All the joy and hope from our evening at the *Twiske* evaporated, replaced by the old and all-too-familiar terror. We heard him stomp round the outside of the house and held our breath, writing for him to smash the window and climb through to get at us. And then, suddenly, and because it was so unexpected, a shocking silence: no breaking glass, no footsteps, no more angry shouts. I looked at Anna; her eyes hard with fear, she stared back at me. Neither of us dared to speak. But eventually we crawled to the door and looked out. The street was waking up, our neighbours making their way to work – but there was no sign of Ricardo. He had gone, presumably frightened off by the early commuter traffic. We had done it. We had escaped.

Or so we thought.

THIRTEEN

Olivia: Escape

My dad was woken by a gun pressed against his temple. Two men, dressed in dark clothes and black gloves, their faces hidden by masks, pulled him out of bed, pistol-whipped his head and bound his hands with plastic cable ties. Then they demanded money.

It was 2 November 2006, almost four months since I had walked away from Ricardo, vowing never to have any contact with him again. Although I was still selling my body in the windows, I was working for myself and no longer had to hand over half of my earnings to my pimp. I felt relieved to have freed myself from him; but now, he was back to take his revenge on my family. And in part, at least, it was my fault.

Anna and I had continued to work in the Red Light District; we had been renting our bodies for so long that we now saw ourselves as nothing more than sexual servants and, even if we had known another way to make a living, we had neither the self-belief nor strength to see a way out of prostitution.

Curiously, although Ricardo had walked past our windows every night, deliberately letting us know he was there and glowering at us, he never made any attempt to speak to us. We were, in truth, surprised that he seemed to have accepted so easily the loss of the two girls he had completely dominated for more than five years; the women he had forced into the windows and whose earnings had provided him with hundreds of thousands of euros.

We assumed that he must have found another victim – or, more likely, victims – and that their bodies were now supporting his lifestyle. That, certainly, was the word on the cobbled streets of De Wallen. But we also realised that my friendship with Elijah was a major factor; Ricardo was always too afraid to challenge the major players in Amsterdam's criminal underworld, and this dealer was one of the biggest fish in that dirty sea. And so we counted on our association with him, coupled with his reputation for serious criminal connections, to protect us.

I should have known better. I should have realised that it was not in Ricardo's nature to let any perceived slight go unpunished, and certainly not to give up such a lucrative meal ticket without so much as a whimper. All through the summer and into early autumn anger and resentment boiled inside him, and he plotted a way to take his revenge.

Although I had been determined not to allow him back into our lives in any way, as the months passed without incident, I became a little too complacent, and in October I briefly let my guard down. The immediate cause was the car he had made me buy for him. It was a little blue Opel Astra hatchback – a far cry from the flashy, blinged-out 'pimp mobiles' owned by his rivals from the larger Turkish or Yugoslavian gangs and which were a familiar sight in De Wallen; nonetheless, Ricardo was evidently determined to drive as though it could match their horsepower and ostentation. The result was an inevitable and seemingly endless succession of speeding tickets which, since he had insisted the car had to be registered in my name rather than his, were legally my responsibility

Each fine was between €250 and €300 and, when we still lived in the flat together, I had regularly tried to get him either to drive more responsibly or to pay the penalty charges himself. Invariably, he refused and pressing the point resulted in another beating. But now that I was free of him – and since he seemed to have accepted this – I decided I should no longer have to pay out thousands of euros a month for his reckless-ness. And so at the end of October, I called his phone and told him it was time he registered the car in his own name.

Again, he took the news surprisingly calmly. We made an appointment for him to come to the house a few days' later so that we could go to Post Office together and sign the transfer papers. I should have guessed it was the opening he had been waiting for.

I was in the shower when he arrived. I let him in and told him to wait while I got ready; he was suspiciously friendly and accommodating, and offered to sort out the documenta-tion on his own. Naïvely, I turned my back on him and went back to finish washing; as soon as I was out of the room, he took the opportunity to steal a key I had left sitting on a little table. The key was to the front door of my dad's house. Unbeknownst to me at the time, Ricardo took it to a shop in the city, had a copy made and then slipped the original back through our door, along with the documents confirming the car was now registered in his name.

My parents were then going through one of their frequent periods of brief separation. As usual they had argued violently and my mum had walked out and gone to stay with her relatives. Which was why, at the start of November, my dad was alone in their house when Ricardo and one of his Surinamese cousins used the duplicate key to let themselves in.

From living with me, Ricardo knew that my dad had a good job and was likely to keep some cash at home, but I'm sure he also suspected I had been sending some of my earnings over to his house for safe keeping. He shoved the gun into my dad's startled face, then beat him with the barrel before dragging him across the floor, ordering him to hand over all the money in the house. He threatened to kill him if he refused. My dad believed he meant it, and showed Ricardo where to find the €1,100 in cash that he had in the house. However, Ricardo made it clear that this wasn't enough; he had expected to find a much larger sum of cash, so to compensate he helped himself to my dad's wallet and credit cards.

Even for a man whose own willingness to use violence had blighted my family's life, it must have been a terrifying ordeal for my dad. To be robbed, at gunpoint, brutally beaten and left tied up in his own home was far beyond any aspect of the comfortable middle-class life he was used to. But it was also a particularly stupid crime. Although Ricardo wore a mask to disguise his face, Dad recognised the voice demanding money; three years earlier the same person had sat in front of him, claiming that Anna and I had asked him to be our pimp. When he managed to free himself from the cable ties, Dad phoned the police, and then he called me.

It was 4.30 a.m. and Anna and I were asleep. More accurately, we were sedated; the previous day had been our one night off from the windows and we had, by then, become dependent on powerful tranquilisers to knock us out. (It's a measure of how intertwined our lives had become with the trade in illegal narcotics that we got these pills from Elijah, who in turn got them from a psychiatrist to whom he supplied regular quantities of drugs.)

I was groggy when the call came, but when I heard the fear and urgency in my dad's voice I quickly woke up. He told me he had been beaten and robbed and said that he thought my pimp – my ex-pimp, as I corrected him – was responsible. If so, both Anna and I were now in grave danger; he ordered us to get out of our house immediately in case Ricardo came looking for us and the extra cash he had expected to find in Dad's home. We arranged to go straight to the police station and to meet him there.

Before he hung up, he asked for the make and registration number of Ricardo's car; he knew that the sooner he gave that to the police, the greater the chance that Ricardo would be caught in possession of the incriminating evidence.

There are only two main roads between my family's village and Amsterdam. The main route is the motorway that runs into the centre of the city, but, working on a hunch, the police guessed that Ricardo would take the less popular A road which loops round through the suburb of Zaandam; especially at that time in the early hours, it would offer a quieter and less visible get away. Their instinct was right.

I have a copy of the police report in front of me as I write. In plain, unemotional language it records my dad's report of an armed robbery, and the action taken by two brave plain-clothes cops. They had very little to go on other than Dad's recollection that one of the raiders wore white sports shoes – and that they might be driving a blue Opel Astra. The officers, driving an unmarked police vehicle, began searching for it along the almost deserted road leading into Amsterdam.

Within a few minutes they saw a car matching the description speed past them; a check on its licence plate showed that it had recently been registered to Ricardo, and that there was a lengthy record of motoring offences and fines associated with the vehicle. They began to pursue it from a safe distance, aware that if this was the robbers' car, at least one of them was armed with an automatic weapon.

A few kilometres outside Zaandam, the Astra pulled into a service station. The cops followed it in and noted that the occupants were two dark-skinned males. The driver got out, filled the tank with petrol then walked to the shop to pay; his companion also left the car, heading for the toilet at the back of the building.

The officers seized the opportunity. They ran over to the car and very quickly found my dad's wallet and his credit cards beneath the front passenger seat, but there was no sign of the cash – or of the gun. They arrested Ricardo the moment he emerged from the shop, then waited for his accomplice. When he returned from relieving himself, they snapped handcuffs over his wrists and checked his pockets; they found €1175, a handful of cable ties and pair of black gloves, but still no weapon. At that point coppers' instinct must have kicked in because one of officers went to search the toilet block. When he returned, he had the black automatic pistol in an evidence bag. Ricardo's cousin had unsuccessfully tried to hide it in the cistern.

When my dad phoned to tell me the news that Ricardo had been taken into custody and would be charged with armed robbery, I was overwhelmed by a succession of conflicting emotions. The first was elation: the man who had dominated the last five years of my life, who had beaten Anna and me, raped me and forced us into sexual servitude would, at last, be brought to justice. Assuming he was convicted – and given the evidence, it seemed inevitable – he would be given a substantial prison sentence; even a country as tolerant as Holland punished crimes like his severely. That meant we would, at last, be free of him and of the long shadow of fear he had cast over us.

This euphoria was quickly replaced by a profound sense of shame. I did not have a good relationship with my mum and dad, and still felt a lingering resentment for my troubled childhood and what – in my view – it had led to. But nothing they had done – or not done – deserved the ordeal that had been inflicted on my dad. That, to a very large degree, was my fault; it was my association with Ricardo which had ultimately caused this terrible crime. I felt culpable, dirty and ashamed.

But I also felt angry. Although I was thankful for the two plain-clothes cops and the speed with which they had caught Ricardo, the more I thought about it, the more I was outraged that he had been allowed to stay free for so long. When he tried to strangle me on the industrial estate, I had begged the police to charge him; if they had listened to me then, taken me seriously instead of dismissing me as just another Red Light District whore moaning about her pimp, he would never have had have the chance to shove a gun in my dad's face.

The next day I went down to the police station to make a statement. The detective who interviewed me wrote down the details of my involvement with Ricardo and how he had stolen the key to my parents' house. But I also made him record that I had previously complained about being coerced into prostitution and demanded that violent pimping be added to the charges.

The officer's response was depressing. He asked if I was still working in the windows and if so, was I currently being forced to sell sex. The answer to that second question was, of course, no: Anna and I had stopped working for Ricardo four months earlier – and that, apparently, meant that nothing could be done. It didn't seem to matter that we had originally been forced into the windows and kept there by frequent beatings; we were now, in the eyes of the law, willingly prostituting ourselves. The best he could offer was that my statement would be kept on file.

Looking back, that moment was both a terrible missed opportunity and, though it would not come for almost a year, the beginning of the end. Had the police opened an investigation into Ricardo's activities as a vicious pimp, I am sure that this would have helped Anna and I to begin the long, difficult journey out of the commercial sex trade. Their refusal to do so reinforced our feelings of worthlessness and impotence; we took it as a sign that no one actually cared enough to help us out of the glass prison to which we had been condemned. That our jailor, the man who had groomed and forced us into it, was now safely behind bars of his own, was not the point. Our captivity was now a psychological one; we had been groomed, beaten and then programmed as prostitutes and we simply could not see a way to escape from this life. And so we continued to serve our sentence, continued to open our mouths and spread our legs eight or ten times a night for men whose disposable income gave them the legal right to exploit our bodies.

It took until the spring of 2007, and the confluence of three particular incidents, before I found the strength even to think about leaving the Red Light District. The initial spur was Ricardo's trial. After a short hearing in which the evidence was laid out in all its damning detail, he and his cousin were convicted of armed robbery and each sentenced to four-year prison terms.

It's hard to convey the enormous relief Anna and I experienced when we heard the news. Even with time off for good behaviour – assuming he was capable of that – Ricardo would be locked up for at least two years; no longer would we have to look over our shoulders as we trudged between our flat and our windows in De Wallen, fearing that he would be watching, waiting, planning to re-establish his control over us. We felt – finally – free of him.

We were not, though, free of the existence to which he had condemned us. We were now twenty-one-years old. We had been full-time, full-service prostitutes for three years. Six times a week, 300 nights a year – over 7,000 customers.

Our bodies, strangely, had grown accustomed to this constant demand. Our minds, however, were a very different story.

I had begun to experience severe mental breakdowns. At first they were irregular and came at seemingly random intervals; the depression hit out of the blue, then disappeared as fast as it had come, leaving me free of it for a couple of months. But by that spring of 2007 they had become frequent; every four weeks, and then every two, I was struck down with feelings of loss and loneliness so deep and debilitating that I felt myself disappearing into an abyss of self-loathing that left me unable to perform anything more than the essential functions. Washing and dressing became towering, barren mountains requiring every ounce of my strength to climb; eating was no more than a task I forced myself to accomplish in order to replenish my dwindling reserves of physical energy. Lethargy began as an occasional symptom of my condition, then became my default state of being.

It was in a period when I had managed to haul myself out of one of these troughs that, for the first time in my life, I began a real, adult romantic relationship. It turned out to be the second in the trinity of events that led to my escape from the windows.

In the months since our date in the *Twiske*, I had occasionally met up with Roger. He was sweet and kind and I enjoyed his company, but, in the end, our dates were just that: brief, pleasant, but ultimately not serious. By the time we turned 22, in April 2007, it dawned on me that neither Anna nor I had ever had a real boyfriend; while other girls of our age were finding long-term partners and experiencing the joy of decent and caring love, we had been fully occupied with providing brief, transactional sexual services to men who never even troubled to ask our names.

On one of our nights off, we went to a bar for drinks and dinner. For us this was a treat, an oasis of normality in our otherwise bleak existence; it felt good to be part of a world in which men and women met on equal terms, talking, laughing, even flirting honestly and openly. In the course of the evening I found myself being chatted up by a good-looking athletic man of my own age and – another first – actually enjoying the experience. My new friend was a professional football player; he was funny, interesting and attractive and at the end of the evening we went home together.

At first he didn't know I was working in the windows; I was too embarrassed to tell him how I earned my living, too fearful that it would scare him off. But it proved impossible to keep this secret for long, and one night he called me to say that he had found out I was a prostitute and that, to protect his reputation, he had to break up with me. When he said this, he wasn't angry or hostile, but rather horribly, painfully sad. But he was also adamant: for as long as I rented my body to other men, he could not be my boyfriend.

That was a breakthrough for me, a sign. Although it hadn't worked out with the footballer, on a night off in a bar a few months later I met someone else – a kind, decent guy who cared for me as a person. Thomas helped me understand that working in the windows was not normal; that not every man wanted a woman to be nothing more than a sex toy, a commodity to be bought and discarded whenever the mood took them. Some men – and he was one of them – were seeking real love, with all the commitment and complexities this involved. We began what would turn out to be an eight-year relationship.

Thomas was twenty-eight – six years older than me – and I found myself falling in love with him. He was kind, gentle, and compassionate; he patiently helped me to confront the truth that prostitution was slowly killing me and wrecking any chance I might have of one day finding a good, normal life. With his support I realised that I had to stop. I had to get out. The only question was how.

The Red Light District was the only world I knew. I had entered it the moment I became legally old enough to do so, and since then I had gained no real experience of any other working environment. I certainly had none of what businesses outside termed transferrable skills: I had no school diplomas, no college degree, no resumé that I could show to potential employers. Which is why it seemed natural to look *inside* De Wallen's borders – and how I came to make another bad life choice.

There are really only two major industries in the Red Light District: sex and drugs. To leave the former, I had to get into bed with the latter – and if this was escaping the frying pan for the false sanctuary of the fire, well, I was still too lost to realise the mistake. I turned, then, to the man who had protected me from Ricardo; I asked Elijah, my friend the coke dealer, for a job.

I can't say I'm proud of this. I know now the devastation illegal drugs can cause – to those who take them and to their families. I also know I should have understood this then. All I can ask you to accept is that difficult dilemmas often lead to bad choices. And I made one.

Elijah had a lucrative business. As well as catering to tourists in De Wallen and supplying the needs of the trafficked women for regular fixes, he also had a large number of customers outside Amsterdam. This inevitably involved a fair amount of driving round the countryside, delivering drugs as and when they phoned for a score; to meet the demands this imposed on his daily routine, he hired me as his chauffeur.

Despite the nature of our cargo, I enjoyed the job. Elijah had always been kind to me; he never asked for any sexual contact or favours, never once laid a finger on me. And he was pleasant company – we always had interesting conversations in which he patiently gave me genuinely good advice on what I could do in the future – which made our journeys fun. He was also a generous employer, paying me good wages; although these, were, of necessity, always handed over in cash. I didn't give the implications much thought. Like all the other women in the windows, I had never paid a penny piece in tax on my prostitution earnings, so I don't think it occurred to me that taking payment for enabling illegal drug deals was a distinctly risky proposition.

The truth is that, for the first time in my twenty-two years on the planet, it felt good to be alive. I was young, evidently worth more than a €50 suck and fuck, and I had a handsome, caring boyfriend to prove it. In contrast to every other man I had known, he treated me with respect and kindness.

But above all I had escaped from the glass prison into which Ricardo had forced me on my eighteenth birthday. I was no longer a prostitute, no longer required to satisfy the selfish lusts of eight to ten men a night.

The one dark spot on this seemingly bright landscape was Anna. She had not been as lucky as me: there was no good-looking lover in her life, and Elijah didn't need another assistant. For all my new-found happiness, I knew that she was my truest and only real friend, and that she remained trapped in the windows. I saw, every evening, the terrible toll this was taking. I realised that one day soon it would break her completely.

And so I hoped, I prayed, that she too would find a similar way out of the Red Light District, and that when that time came, I could help her. I should, I see now, have been a little more careful about what I wished for.

FOURTEEN

Anna: Choices

April 2008. I was twenty-three years old. I had long since given up counting how many men satisfied their lusts inside me but – and this is a conservative estimate – the total must have exceeded 12,000. It could well have been more.

I had been renting my body to these strangers for seven years. For the first five of those, I had no choice. But I had been free of Ricardo's brutal control for almost two years, and yet I remained trapped as a sex slave in the Red Light District. Which begs a simple question: why?

That period is one of the parts of my life which is hardest to explain. I was no longer answerable to a pimp, no longer living in fear of a beating if I dared to refuse the nightly succession of customers who knocked on my window. There was nothing physically to stop me pulling the curtains shut, packing up my belongings, walking away. Does that mean that I was, as the city of Amsterdam likes to portray its sex workers, a willing and entirely voluntary Happy Hooker?

No. No, I wasn't. I hated this work. I dreaded the pain

and degradation inflicted on me every single night; and I loathed the selfish men who took advantage of my presence there. Legally, perhaps, I consented, but by any other civilised standard of human behaviour I was being sexually abused.

But, you say, but, but, but. You didn't protest, Anna; you never really told any of these customers that you didn't want them inside you, you never pleaded with them to give you a break. You never went to the police, never even called out to one of the uniformed cops who cycled past your building every night, or asked for help from one of the Christian outreach groups who occasionally turned up at every prostitute's window, offering succour if not sanctuary. You never said a word. And that is absolutely and horribly true.

Why, then, do I insist I didn't truly consent – not once – throughout that two-year period? The answer is simple. I didn't know *how* to say no. I didn't think that I ever could. The walls that kept me locked up were no longer physical, they were mental. I had been programmed by Ricardo, and by the industry itself, to believe that Anna Hendriks was, and would always be, a sex worker. I had no more value to the world than the price of a suck and fuck – and that made me utterly, hopelessly worthless.

Does that sound extreme? Improbable and even self-pitying? If so, I apologise, but it is the truth.

That was what had happened to Olivia. Elijah's offer of work outside the windows – however ethically questionable it might be – was an intervention that helped her see that she could escape; I needed someone to hold out the same hope to me. A year later, someone did – and, initially at least, in similar circumstances. Unfortunately, my salvation turned out to be temporary and rather more problematic.

One of my mother's brothers owned a 'grow shop' business, selling the equipment needed to raise cannabis plants. It's one of the peculiar quirks of Dutch drug laws that whilst it is legal to buy weed, possess it in small amounts and to smoke it openly, importing or cultivating the drug on a commercial basis is – in theory – strictly forbidden. Quite where the police and government believe the coffeeshops get their supplies from is a mystery, but, nonetheless, the prohibition creates a substantial market for home-grown plants.

My uncle, like the rest of my family, knew that I worked in the windows. He knew, too, that I wasn't doing so from choice and one day, in what he presented as an act of generous philanthropy, told me he had a plan to help me escape. He suggested that we should go into business together, cultivating cannabis on an industrial scale.

It's easy, twelve years later, to see that this scheme was – at best – dubious; more to the point it would involve me in serious criminal activity. Looking back, I want to shake my twenty-three-year-old self and tell her not to be so stupid; to make her question why, after years in which my mother's family had ostracised me, her brother should suddenly offer to come to my rescue. But that's hindsight. At the time all I saw – all I could see – was that it could be a lifeline, the path that would lead me out of prostitution.

And so I agreed. In the middle of 2008, I locked up my room in De Wallen, returned the keys to the rental agency and cancelled our contract. Before I walked away, I took a moment to take a last look back at my prison. A heavy weight lifted from my mind as I realised that I would no longer have to work within its cold, bare walls, lie down on its shabby bed or pace its grimy floor. My time in the windows was finally over; my sentence was served and never again would I have to rent my tired body for the pleasure of strangers. For the first time in seven years, I experienced an emotion I had believed lost to me: I felt the faintest of stirrings of hope.

My uncle had plainly spent a long time thinking about his scheme and had the whole venture worked out. His role was to be that of a silent partner, putting up all the money needed for premises, seeds and equipment. He would also be responsible for the water and electricity bills we would incur; since we would be growing large numbers of plants indoors these energy costs would be substantial. My job was to be the front woman for the entire enterprise; I was to be the one who, on paper at least, operated the business, in return for which I would reap a share of the profits. I really should have known better.

My very first tasks should have sounded the alarm. We needed to rent a house in which our crop was to be raised; just like the windows agency, the leasing company would require me to present my passport as evidence of my identity. This potentially exposed me to some risk; if, at some point in the future, anyone happened to discover our weed factory, the police would be certain to come looking for me as its apparent owner.

My uncle told me that this was very unlikely to happen and that even if I was caught, nothing really bad would happen; he also promised to pay for a lawyer to defend me and insisted that the worst punishment I could expect would be a short spell of community service. But he had also come up with a plan to protect me. Before I made contact with the leasing agency, he sent me to the police station to file a false report that my passport had been stolen. That way, he explained, if the Amsterdam drug squad ever arrested me, I could claim that someone else had used my missing ID to rent the house. Thefts like this were an occupational hazard for women working in the windows, so although the story was completely untrue, the police duly wrote it down and filed it without asking any questions. I walked out with a copy of the bogus report in my handbag.

But that was only half of the fraud. Unlike the company that rented windows to prostitutes, the agencies that leased entire houses wanted some evidence that prospective tenants could pay the bill; typically they demanded copies of recent wage slips as proof. Whilst this was perfectly reasonable, it posed an obvious problem for me. In seven years I had never been employed by a legitimate business; selling sex in the Red Light District windows was strictly a cash-only operation, and even the part-time work I had done as a young teenager had been on a casual, no questions asked, basis.

My uncle had evidently foreseen this minor difficulty. Before I made appointments to visit a succession of leasing companies and to view the properties they had available for rent, he handed me a fake pay slip that showed that I had the required history of earning wages. It is, I think, an indication of my desperate need to get out of the Red Light District that I recklessly went along with this fraud.

The house I eventually chose was in my old village. I told the estate agent that Olivia and I wanted to move out of

Amsterdam to be closer to our families – another lie, of course: neither of us had any intention of living there, even if the mass of cannabis plants my uncle quickly installed would have left any room to do so. I took out the lease and entered into contracts with the electricity and water companies. Everything was now in my name, but that was the limit of my involvement; as soon as the papers were signed, I handed the house keys over to my uncle and left him to get on with the job of cultivating the first batch of weed.

Marijuana is a fast-growing crop. The time it takes to rear plants from seed to harvest is generally little more than six months. I worked out that with the money I had saved from renting my body, if I took a low-paid job in a bar, Olivia and I could live quite comfortably until the first profits from the weed scheme rolled in. And so, for the first time in years I found myself working for honest and legitimate wages; €5 an hour wasn't much, but it was enough – and it was a relief to be earning money without having to spread my legs.

Half a year passed. I waited for my uncle to phone me with the news that the harvest was in and that I could soon expect my share of the proceeds. The call never came. I was initially not concerned; I enjoyed my part-time work in the bar, I was sharing a nice apartment in Amsterdam with Olivia and finally my life felt good. But as more weeks, and then months, passed without news I realised that something was wrong. I called my uncle and demanded to know when I would be paid.

He had, I would later discover, anticipated my call, and had prepared a story that the first crop had failed but that another was coming along nicely; I just had to be patient and wait a little while longer. More weeks passed, more phone calls, and always the same response: there was a problem with the plants, there was no harvest and, eventually, he told me there was to be no payday – ever. With that, he washed his hands of the whole wretched business.

I put the phone down and looked at Olivia. Both of us were stunned. However foolishly, we had invested all our hopes for the future in the weed factory and now that those dreams had been snatched away we realised we would soon be unable to pay the rent on our flat. But very quickly our shock turned to anger. Once again, or so it seemed to us, we had been screwed; once again I had been exploited by a man who pretended to care – and this time it was a relative, not a violent pimp, who took advantage of my naïvety.

Within weeks the problem turned into a full-blown disaster. Bills for the costs of running the cannabis nursery started to land on the doormat of our flat in Amsterdam; the first was from the electricity company for €10,000, rapidly followed by an invoice for the water and then – most alarming of all – a law suit from the leasing agency.

The owner of the house had somehow discovered that it was being used to cultivate substantial quantities of marijuana plants. He jumped to the conclusion – not unreasonably, I suppose – that the whole operation was part of a large-scale drug syndicate and that I was fronting for an organized crime gang. He promptly filed a legal claim, demanding €90,000 compensation. He also reported me to the police.

Even then I was less worried than I should have been. After all, the business really belonged to my uncle, and he had promised to pay all the costs as well as to hire a lawyer to defend me. It didn't turn out that way.

I arranged to meet him and asked him to keep his end of the bargain. His reaction was blunt and contemptuous. He claimed the cannabis nursery had been my idea and refused to take any responsibility for any of the utility bills – let alone the landlord's huge compensation claim. Then he warned me against giving evidence against him; with a smile on his face, he told me that if I passed his name to the police, he would inform them that I was drug-addicted prostitute, a junkie whore from the Red Light District, and that consequently no one would believe my story.

I thought I had lost the capacity for shock; I thought that seven years of being used by thousands of strangers had effectively cauterised the part of my brain that processed pain or surprise. I was wrong. Nothing – not Ricardo's beatings nor the humiliation of sexual slavery – had prepared me for such duplicity by a close family member. I had known my uncle all my life; in the years after my father abandoned us, he and my mother's other brothers had helped raise me. How could he now so casually – so cynically – betray me? The fragile bubble of hope in which I had been living since escaping from prostitution evaporated. There was worse to come.

I plucked up enough courage to talk to my mother. Although we had barely spoken in recent years, I thought that she would have enough residual feeling for her only child at least to listen. She did not. Instead, she took my uncle's side, insisting that she accepted his story that he hadn't instigated the weed-factory business, had never made any money from it in any event, and that, unlike me, he was a good and decent person. All my problems were, she said, of my own making; I had made my bed – an unpleasant reminder of my previous occupation – and now I must lie in it.

My father proved similarly unhelpful. Initially he agreed to help me hire a lawyer and to try and negotiate a deal with the owner of the house; neither promise materialised. Instead it was Olivia's parents who found me a solicitor and who took both of us to meet him. Olivia had been party to almost all of the arrangements between my uncle and I, so we assumed the lawyer would need to take a statement from her. Wrong – again.

He told us that I had nothing to worry about. There was little chance, he promised me, that I would be taken to court for the simple reason that since I had never held a regular job – one that paid wages which the legal system could assess – there would be no realistic way to impose a compensation order on me. I can still remember the exact phrase he used in delivering this complacent reassurance: 'They can't pick feathers off a bald chicken.'

He did, though, give us two pieces of useful information. The first was that if I wanted to remain, to use his analogy, unpluckable, I should quit my part-time job in the bar; in the unlikely event that the case did proceed, and that I lost, the meagre wages it paid could be seized to pay off my debt. I found it hard to process the implications of this: it seemed to suggest that I could be punished for undertaking honest work, but that money I made from the miserable business of renting my body was untouchable. It made little logical sense.

The second news was that my uncle had doubly deceived me. The lawyer showed us official documents which indicated that the weed crop had not failed; instead it had yielded a beneficent harvest – worth between €150,000 and €200,000, according to police estimates. That apparently explained why the landlord had sued for such a large sum of money.

Despite the lawyer's assurances, the case continued, and I ended up in court. Since all the documents – the house lease, the contracts for electricity and water – were in my name, the result was inevitable. The landlord won and I was ordered to pay him €63,500 – the cost, or so he claimed, of repairing damage caused by all the hydroponic growing equipment my uncle had installed in the building. Because I didn't have this substantial sum of money, I was required to pay it off in annual instalments of €4,500.

I had absolutely no way – no *legitimate* way – to do this and simultaneously house and feed myself. Even if I got another bar job, my wages would be, at best, €5 an hour – and even that would be largely seized to meet the terms of the court's order. There was, at least as far as I could see, only one way I, a twenty-three-year-old woman with no qualifications or employment history, could earn enough to repay my debt. I would have to return to the windows.

Tell me: was this a choice? Was I voluntarily going back to selling my body? Was I consenting, doing so of my own free will? Technically, by the strict letter of the law, I suppose the answer is yes. No one put a gun to my head; there was no violent pimp or crew of violent gangsters forcing me to walk back into the glass prison from which I had managed to escape. But in truth, in reality, I don't believe I had any genuine choice. The court said the debt had to be repaid; it may not have used fists or a weapon, but in effect its order was just as much my pimp as Ricardo had once been.

I wish I could find a way to convey what this did to my mind. Depression, despair, a sense of utter bleakness – none of these words come anywhere close to describing the psychological toll of knowing that I would once again be forced to offer my body up on a conveyor belt. I had glimpsed hope, and it had been snatched away from me. Yet even in my worst moments of desolation, I was able to appreciate a bitter irony: because the Dutch government didn't – then – tax the earnings of prostitutes, the court would not know I had money to be seized. If I paid off the debt – and, for what little remained of my sense of self-esteem, I was determined to comply with the judgment against me – I would be doing so voluntarily. That, at least, was a choice I could make for myself.

There was only one consolation in the whole miserable affair, and, true to form, it was bitter-sweet. When I told Olivia of my decision, she held me close and told me that she wouldn't let me do this alone. 'Your debt is my debt,' she said simply. It was an extraordinary act of sacrifice and one which showed just how much she loved me. And from a purely practical point of view, the debt would be paid off much more quickly with both of us working.

So at the end of 2008, we both returned to the windows of the Red Light District. It would take almost another full year before we could escape again. But when we did, this time it was for ever.

FIFTEEN

Olivia: Justice

District Court, 2011

He glared at us across the courtroom. His eyes were hard and black with hatred; his body tensed as if ready to leap out of his seat in the dock and rush over to administer another punishment beating for daring to bring him so low.

We had been told we didn't need to see him, that we could give our evidence via a secure video-link from a room safely outside his reach. Anna would have taken this option if I'd let her, but I refused. I was determined to confront the man who had ruled and ruined our lives; I wanted to look into his vicious, arrogant face and make him hear the cost of everything he had done to us. I wanted justice – oh God, I longed for that – but most of all I wanted to see justice being done. And I wanted him to see me. I savoured the sweet taste of revenge.

It was a Friday in 2011: eleven years since Ricardo had wormed his way into our lives, ten since he had first pimped

Anna to his Iranian customer, and eight since he had forced both of us into the windows of the Red Light District. Now, at last, he was on trial: a defendant in the dock, charged with violent pimping and human trafficking. This was the end of our dark, miserable journey and I wasn't going to be intimidated or forced to hide from him any longer. I wouldn't have missed a single second in that courtroom.

The road that brought Anna and I to the district court that summer's morning had been long and difficult. We had finally managed to get out of De Wallen almost two years earlier, but escaping from the sex industry's coils had proved to be one of the hardest paths either of us had ever walked.

From the moment we returned to the windows at the end of 2008 – the only way we could then see to pay off Anna's fines for her uncle's dope-factory scheme – we struggled, emotionally, physically and, to our dismay, financially. Our previous experience had conditioned us to believe that, however much we loathed doing it, by selling our bodies we would quickly earn enough money to clear the debt. But we discovered that we were being forced back into prostitution at the worst possible time. The rental agency had greatly increased the cost of hiring a room – up 50 per cent to €150 per night – just at the moment that the Amsterdam tourist trade, the great tide of travellers on which the legal prostitution industry depended, was hit by the international financial crisis. With the world's economy staggering from the collapse of banks in the United States, Britain and across Europe, there was a noticeable reduction in the number of visitors making their way to the Red Light District – and a very definite new awareness of the price of our services.

But this was not solely the result of the global economic downturn. At the same time, international sex traffickers were shipping an ever-greater number of women – primarily from the former Soviet states, the Far East and Central Africa – to fill the neon-lit windows of De Wallen.

In 2010 – just over a year after we returned to prostitution – Holland's national trafficking organization, COMENSHA, recorded 800 new sex slaves brought into the country by organized crime gangs. And these women were unquestionably slaves; we had seen them and worked – or tried to work – in the rooms next to them. They were often much younger than Anna and I, barely the age at which Ricardo had forced us into the commercial sex trade. And they were terrified – brutalised, isolated and, often as not, strung out on drugs.

The men who shipped them in were gangs with a keen understanding of the economics of the trade in flesh. Legalised prostitution meant that there would always be a demand for sexual services in Amsterdam, even in times of financial hardship; like all 'good' businessmen they knew that the two key requirements for making serious money were limiting overheads and undercutting the prices of rival 'providers'. The first was easy. The women they exploited were either tricked or forced by extreme violence into the trade; the only cost to the organisations which pimped them were the limited expenses of driving them across the border and bribing whatever official needed a kickback to ease their passage.

The second element was pure free-market capitalism. With customers feeling the financial pinch and increasingly willing to demand more for their money than the usual perfunctory

€50 suck and fuck, the gangs simply ordered their slaves to offer more exotic fare at reduced prices: condom-free sex, once a non-negotiable taboo, quickly moved from being an optional extra to be paid for to a routine expectation.

The trafficked women had no choice in this: refusing a customer – however extreme or dangerous his demands – would earn them a swift and brutal beating. Anna and I, working for ourselves (albeit under what we saw as duress), continued to refuse to put our bodies at any more risk than was absolutely necessary. The result was inevitable.

Throughout the ten months in which we tried to pay off the debt, we found ourselves losing out to the victims of sexual trafficking imprisoned in the windows around us. To cash-conscious customers they were cheaper, more flexible in terms of what they would do for less money, and, frankly, too scared to complain. There were nights – and they became increasingly frequent – when we failed to earn even enough to pay the room rental bill. In our experience, the Red Light District had never been a safe, well-regulated space for women to willingly open their mouths and legs in exchange for a fistful of euros, but from 2009 it turned darker, wilder and even more lawless. We began to feel a sense of very real danger in the cobbled streets beside the canals.

We had good reason to do so. Very soon after we returned to prostitution, a familiar face reappeared: Ricardo. Although he had been sentenced to four years in prison for the robbery on my father, he had, as is normal, been released on licence after two. He used his freedom to re-establish himself as a pimp and small-time gang-leader in the Red Light District; by the time we were back in the windows, he was a constant presence on its streets. Often he had with him a very young-looking girl; evidently he had found a new victim to prey on.

That was bad enough; we watched, heartbroken, knowing that this young girl was undergoing exactly what he had put us through for so long. But Ricardo was also determined to take revenge for our part in his robbery conviction. He patrolled up and down the cobbles, glowering at us until one night he tricked his way into Anna's room.

He knew that neither of us would ever let him in, so he sent one of his henchmen to pose as a customer; when Anna unlocked the door, the thug stepped aside and Ricardo marched in. He leered at her and told her that he knew where we lived and that we went home alone and unprotected by any other pimp; the message was clear – one night he would come for us.

Our situation was, we began to see, a perfect storm. Higher rents, greater competition, lower prices and, always in the background, the threat of a vicious beating – or, quite possibly, murder. Both of us sank once again beneath the weight of our despair and a lowering shroud of depression. Although we still had the debt to pay, we knew we could not continue to rent our bruised bodies, or to subject our damaged minds to much more trauma; the question, though, was how to escape, how to quit?

It sounds so simple when I type those words; after all, no one was pointing a gun at our heads, much less shoving it in our mouths, to make us stay in the windows. If anything, we were risking our lives by remaining there, so how difficult could it be to just walk away?

The answer is that it was very difficult indeed. The truth – the unspoken truth – about the legalised prostitution industry is that getting out of the sex trade is much, much harder than being forced into it.

Neither of us had any qualifications; nor did we have any self-esteem. Our only worth – or so it seemed – was as pieces of meat, to be used and abused by the men who rented our bodies; and so the 'real' world, with its complex dynamics of normal day-to-day interactions that most people take for granted, was a terrifying prospect. To find our way into this normal life, we needed to get completely away from everything that surrounded us: the sex, the violence and the drugs. And for that, we needed professional help.

For a city – and, indeed a country (because other Dutch municipalities have followed Amsterdam and licenced their own Red Light Districts) – which earns so much from the sex industry, there is surprisingly little official effort to aid those who try to escape from prostitution. We discovered that there were just two organisations that helped women like us find the immense strength and support needed to leave the business. We sought assistance from both of them.

The first, *De Rode Draad* (it means 'The Red Thread') focused almost exclusively on supporting women who had been trafficked into Amsterdam from outside Holland; because we were Dutch and not – yet – viewed as trafficking victims, it regretfully told us that it could not offer any help. The door to exit number one was slammed in our faces.

The second organization was called *De Scharlaken Koord* – the Scarlet Cord – and at first glance it seemed more promising. Its staff were good, caring and dedicated men and women;

they have operated in De Wallen since 1985, regularly visiting women like us in the windows, bringing food and offering to listen to our stories. It is brave, sometimes dangerous work, since the pimps frequently threaten them with violence and chase them away.

However, the Scarlet Cord is an avowedly Christian organization. I don't want to be unfair – none of its staff were wild-eyed evangelicals, bent on converting us to their religious convictions – but we found its insistence on belief in God very difficult to reconcile with everything we had been through. If, as the people we met there assured us, a benevolent deity held us in his (or, I suppose, her) tender care, how could we have been so victimised, brutalised and exploited? And beyond us, what about the thousands of wretched, drug-dependent trafficked women shipped in to service the selfish sexual appetites of anyone with the cash to abuse them? How – why – could a just God punish women like us, while letting our abusers roam free? Neither Anna nor I could understand and, for all their genuine kindness, no one at *De Scharlaken Koord* could explain it either.

In the end we realised that our best – our only – hope was the same as it had always been: each other. And so, slowly, very slowly, we worked to pull ourselves out of the windows. After each exhausting shift we talked constantly until daylight drove away the night, mulling over possibilities, testing out ideas for a different, a better, way to live. We took on part-time normal jobs – as receptionists and administrative assistants in offices and hotels; anything to earn legal, decent money that didn't involve selling our bodies. Even though these paid only a fraction of what we earned in the windows, it gave us some hope – a fragile but growing belief that we might soon escape. And, eventually, through each other's constant love and support, we eased ourselves out of prostitution and were gradually able to push the pain of our years in the windows to the back of our minds.

In December 2010 a phone call brought it all back. Vice-squad detectives in Zaanstreek-Waterland, a specially designated government and police 'safety region' covering much of the area adjacent to Amsterdam in Noord Holland, opened an investigation into human trafficking. Operation LIMASS was created after new reports were submitted about a violent and dangerous pimp with a criminal record for armed robbery: Ricardo.

Those complaints had not come from Anna or I but from his latest victim – the young Dutch girl who, as we later discovered, he had forced into the Red Light District with exactly the same combination of loverboy manipulation and extreme brutality that he had used on us. When they checked his files, the police discovered the details of Ricardo's armed robbery of my dad; but they also found copies of the numerous statements I had made between 2004 and 2005, identifying him as the man who beat, coerced, kicked and punched us into prostitution. Now, six years later, it seemed they were finally willing to investigate. They phoned my dad, who gave them my number.

The call came completely out of the blue. When they asked if I knew this man Ricardo, my immediate reactions were shock and panic: all the trauma we had worked so hard to forget came flooding back on a wave of nausea. But I recovered quickly enough to answer simply, 'Yes, he was my pimp: he forced my friend and I into the Red Light District.'

The detectives explained that they were building a case against him and asked if Anna and I would be willing to work with them. There was no hesitation – I told them that both of us would be very pleased indeed to do all we could to bring our abuser to justice.

It took until the new year before they were ready to interview me and Anna. On 7 January 2011, we went to the police station and were questioned separately for several hours. The detectives were careful and thorough, taking us through every aspect our lives from the age of fifteen, but what surprised me most was how much they knew about Ricardo's activities and gang connections; they asked us about his contacts and henchmen – people we had never heard of – and it was clear that he had been, or still was, part of a criminal network stretching far beyond anything we had understood. At four o'clock that afternoon, we signed sworn statements and went home, buoyed by promises that the vice squad was determined to put a stop to his crimes once and for all.

But justice, it seemed, was a very slow-moving process. Weeks passed, then months and – to our intense frustration – there was still no sign of a trial. To their credit, the police kept in contact, updating us on progress in the case, but what we wanted to hear – what, by now, had become an overwhelming psychological need – was the date on which Ricardo would appear in the dock.

Finally, I received a call from the liaison team. They told me that he had been charged with several counts of human trafficking and violent pimping. Six months after we made our sworn statements – we would get our chance to give evidence against him in court.

The criminal charges were brought primarily under the anti-sex trafficking provisions of the Dutch Criminal Code. Introduced shortly after the country legalised prostitution, this specifically recognised the need to protect vulnerable young girls from loverboy-type grooming as well as outright coercion, and its provisions exactly matched the facts of what Ricardo had done to us. But the law had an additional – and unique – feature: it allowed us simultaneously to bring a civil case against him, and for the court to combine this with his criminal trial.

This was an innovative and pioneering approach, since it ensures that women like Anna and I only had to give our evidence – something that every victim of sexual abuse finds deeply distressing – once, rather than at two separate hearings. And, assuming the case against him was proved, as well as sending him to prison, the judges would order him to pay us damages for what he had done. Better still – since thugs like Ricardo are very good at hiding their assets and claiming to be penniless – the government had also recently brought in a new rule that any financial compensation would be paid initially from official funds, and then reclaimed later from wages earned by convicted offenders after their release.

It was a ground-breaking idea and one which recognised the unique problems faced by women forced into prostitution. But for Anna and I, it also meant that we now needed a lawyer.

Our previous experience – the disastrous advice Anna was given over the weed-factory bills – had not left us with any real confidence in the legal profession, but this time we were very much more fortunate. We were referred to a brave and good-hearted solicitor called Richard Korver; he had just won a famous case on behalf of a group of parents whose children had been sexually abused, and he was a forceful opponent of the prostitution industry. Even more importantly, he was determined to give a voice to a women tricked or trafficked into it, and he readily agreed to represent us.

The trial was to take place outside Amsterdam. The city where the case was heard is beautiful, with cobbled streets and traditional three-storey houses retaining much of its historic character; in complete contrast, the district-court building is a sleek, modernist steel and glass structure, set discreetly down a little cul-de-sac.

Anna and I arrived there early on the morning of the hearing. Other than Richard Korver, only my sister came to support us; neither of our respective sets of parents were sufficiently interested to attend the trial which would show how their daughters had gone from respectable (if slightly delinquent) teenagers to enforced sex workers, trapped behind the glass windows of De Wallen. I suppose we should not have been surprised as by then we had almost no contact with them, but their evident indifference hurt us both greatly.

We were also very nervous; even though Anna knew Ricardo couldn't do anything to us inside the court, she was so scared at the prospect of seeing him again that she began shaking. My emotions were different: as I waited to be called in to speak, I found myself consumed by anger and an over-whelming desire for vengeance. I reached down inside of myself, touched this fury and recognised it as something good and natural; I knew that it would help us through the ordeal of giving our evidence.

We were not, though, the first of Ricardo's victims to be called. The young girl whose complaints had led to the police investigation, testified first – but she was so terrified of him that she did so via video-link from a secure room in a completely different part of the court building. I understood why she needed this reassurance, but I was absolutely determined to look straight into Ricardo's eyes as I described what he had done to us.

And so, when our turn came, we walked into the room, our hearts beating fast but with our heads held high. The prosecutor calmly helped us to tell our story to the judges (there are no juries in Holland) who were hearing the case. We left nothing out.

We explained how Ricardo latched on to us at a time when we were very vulnerable and legally still children; I described his use of sex with me as a technique to groom both of us, and Anna spoke simply and movingly about the night on which he first sold her to the Iranian man.

As our evidence progressed, we found that standing up, speaking the truth about our abuser, was a kind of catharsis. The accounts of what Ricardo had done to us flowed out like a river of poison, leaving us feeling exhausted but somehow cleaner. In the security of the courtroom, I found the courage to speak about the sexually transmitted infection, and the two abortions I had undergone; and both of us detailed the beatings he inflicted on us to maintain his control, as well as the psychological scars caused by being forced to service the sexual demands of thousands of men.

Evidently, we touched a nerve. On several occasions the judges suspended the hearing, retiring to their chambers for a break. I assumed – I think correctly – that they were shocked by our accounts, and especially by the fact that I had been under the age of consent when Ricardo first had sex with me, and needed time to get on top of their emotions. I knew just how they felt.

By contrast, Ricardo's reaction was typically vicious and cynical. As we gave our evidence he glared at us, displaying such overt hatred that the court eventually reprimanded him. Then, when it was his turn to testify, he blamed me and Anna for everything, insisting that it had been our idea to become prostitutes, that we had done so willingly – indeed happily – and that all he had ever done was look after us, valiantly keeping us safe in the violent cesspool of De Wallen.

His arrogance and naked contempt did not go down well. The judges asked him a succession of challenging questions and the prosecutor highlighted differences between his written statement to police and his evidence to the court. When he could neither answer the questions nor explain the discrepancies, it was clear to everyone that he was lying.

Finally, at the end of the trial, the court issued its verdict – guilty on all charges – and the judges sentenced Ricardo to six years in prison. I looked over at Anna; tears were in our eyes. We both made the same calculation at exactly the same time. Ricardo's punishment amounted to exactly the total number of years he had forced Anna and I to open our mouths and legs in the windows of the Red Light District. Six years in jail for six years in hell.

Was this enough? No, not for me – not by a very long way. Not only because he wouldn't actually serve all of his sentence – as before, he would be released on probation halfway through – but because the six years he stole from me and Anna were only part of the story. Our sentence lasted – and would continue to last – much, much longer than that. So no, it didn't even come close to being enough.

But just as we were coming to terms with the verdict in the criminal case, the judges handed down the decision in our civil claim against Ricardo. This, too, was based on a simple mathematical calculation. The police report, presented to the court by the prosecutor, laid out precisely how many nights, over exactly how many years, we had each been forced to work for Ricardo as window prostitutes: 6 days a week, 50 weeks every year for three years, making a total of 900 shifts.

Next to this formula was a second reckoning, setting out the detectives' estimate – one which erred on the side of caution – that during each shift we had earned between €300 to €400. That amounted to €120,000 per year; multiplied by three, the total came to €360,000. Each.

Since Ricardo had taken half of the entire sum – and had done so with the threat of violence constantly in the background – the court ruled that he must pay it back, with interest, as well as an additional compensation award for our ordeal. Anna and I were to receive compensation of €217,500 each.

I couldn't quite believe what I was hearing. Looking at Anna, I could see she felt the same conflicting emotions coursing through her mind. On the positive side there was relief and, if I'm honest, the pure joy of payback: Ricardo was going to prison and the fact that the court ordered such huge compensation suggested that the judges – and, by extension, my government and my country – recognised the terrible cost of what had been done to us. The size of the award also meant that Anna could pay off her debts and we could both afford to pay for the extensive psychological treatment we had realised we desperately needed. But while the compensation was very welcome, did it really bear any relation to the suffering we had been put through?

Were the three years he would actually serve in the relative comfort of a Dutch prison (our penal system, like so much else in public policy, is deliberately progressive and enlightened) really sufficient? Yes, he would lose his freedom, but Ricardo's life behind those bars would be paradise compared to the purgatory we had endured on a nightly basis, and I couldn't see how it would deter other brutal, greedy men from living off the bodies of their female victims.

Ultimately, we decided that, imperfect or otherwise, Ricardo had received some sort of justice and we had helped bring it about. Nine years after he first entered our lives, nine years after he had broken us physically and mentally, we were free. Anna and I looked at each other and smiled – we knew then that our ordeal was finally over.

SIXTEEN

Anna: Now

Amsterdam City Centre, Summer 2019

Olivia and I do not live together, but we meet here, in my apartment, every day. This modest third-floor flat, on the edge of the museum district, looks out over one of the city's prettiest canals; it is only just over a kilometre from De Wallen, but it seems like a world away from the filth and corruption of the Red Light District. For the past five years it has been our refuge; a quiet, safe space in which we have slowly rebuilt our lives.

What do those lives look like now? On the surface they are positive and hopeful. Although the legal process dragged on for two more years, and our compensation was dramatically reduced on appeal – I received €42,500 and Olivia got €47,500 – the award enabled us to be completely debt-free; we pooled our money to pay off my fines and used the remainder to support ourselves. Both of us have managed to find and, despite occasional periods of unemployment, hold on to normal jobs in the everyday world. We work in offices, hotels – anywhere that will employ two thirty-three-year-old women with no academic qualifications. The wages are comparatively low and the hours are long, but the rewards are an honest tiredness and the knowledge that what we do to earn a living will not harm us, or anyone else. Our old existence – we cannot bring ourselves to think of the misery of sexual servitude as a 'life' – is behind us. Over. Done.

But it is not forgotten. Because the reality for both of us is that we will never completely escape from the Red Light District. We may no longer have to rent ourselves in its windows, but our bodies still show the physical evidence of our years as prostitutes. Look closely and you can see the deep scars Ricardo inflicted during his frequent beatings; they, like the tattoo which he forced Olivia to have inked on her arm – the mark that showed the world she 'belonged' to him – will never fully disappear. But beneath these superficial disfigurements is something much more severe and insidious: deep and tangled skeins of psychological scar tissue that have proved resistant to healing.

As part of the legal proceedings we were sent to see a psychiatrist; not surprisingly, the court wanted a professional assessment of the mental damage caused by our years of enforced prostitution. The doctor's report was blunt: both of us suffer from post-traumatic stress disorder, are haunted by panic attacks and frequently paralysed by flashbacks to our ordeal in the windows.

We have tried to rid ourselves of this. After receiving the compensation money, we booked ourselves a course of EMDR treatment. Eye Movement Desensitisation and Reprocessing therapy was developed by an American clinical psychologist in the 1980s as a way of identifying and making safe the suffering which the mind has been unable to process. It utilises both physiological and psychological techniques, and is the most advanced and successful clinical tool to repair severely broken minds.

Yet although we found the sessions helpful to combat our anxiety and panic attacks, even they were eventually unable to fix our mental block. The most traumatic moments in our years as Ricardo's victims remain stubbornly impervious to all attempts at retrieval.

If that is terrifying – and barely a day passes without it casting a very dark shadow over us – it is also horribly isolating. Because we can't recall these incidents, we can't talk to anyone about them; it is impossible to explain to an outsider the reason for our sudden and debilitating panic attacks when we cannot dredge up the details for ourselves. In those moments, we only have each other to cling to and to rely on.

The most profound impact is in our emotional responses to those who try to get close to us. Today, both Olivia and I have partners, but it very difficult for these relationships to be normal and entirely healthy. Part of this is, of course, about trust; our boundaries have been so grossly stretched and tested by men that we find it impossible to believe we can be safe in their company. However much our boyfriends tell us that they love us, understand what we went through and that we can rely on them, in the back of our minds there is always the voice of bitter experience warning that we have heard these lies before. And we know where believing in false promises eventually led us: to the Red Light District windows. We have done so much, been forced so low: is it any real surprise that neither of us can ever fully love a man?

Ultimately, I have come to see that this obstacle is founded on the most fundamental requirement for trust. In strong, nourishing relationships, a woman's partner is her best friend. Because of what we have been through together, Olivia and I reserve that bond for each other. No man will ever be able to match the love we share, and that is a major problem that undermines the lives we have with our partners. It is one that they find very difficult to understand. We look like grown women, yet we don't feel that way; inside, deep down, we remain children – the young girls whose adolescence was stolen; we are like embryonic adults, forever frozen in the septic amber of Ricardo's grooming and the commercial sex trade. Because of that, only Olivia understands me, and only I fully grasp what it means to be her.

This, nine years after we left the Red Light District and five since the final verdict in the Court of Appeal, is the reality of our lives. More than that, it is the reality of the true cost of prostitution – and it is why we decided we had to write this book.

It is almost two decades since our country legalised the commercial trade in women's bodies. Since then, scholarly reports and academic books have debated the pros and cons of the decision; the debate has turned into a bitter fight with advocates for either side loudly proclaiming rival arguments. In all of the noise and vitriol, the voices no one hears are those of the women on whose labour – on whose pain and suffering – the entire industry is built. Women like us.

Neither of us pretend to have a perfect answer to the difficult questions posed by legalised prostitution. But we do have something unique: we have personal experience – years of it – which has given us an understanding of how girls like us arrive in the windows of the Red Light District, and of the true price to them of selling sex.

Prostitution is a fact of life. It exists, as it always has, in every country on the planet, and it will continue so long as men have the financial power to indulge their desires with women whose position is either economically, socially or physically vulnerable. But it seems obvious to us that there is a vast and important difference between accepting as reality that men will always seek to purchase their pleasure from those in desperate need of money, and turning this unfairness into an organised, legalised industry – a commercial conveyor belt on which women's bodies are systematically abused and exploited for profit.

We know the arguments in favour of legalising prostitution: that, well regulated and properly policed, Red Light Districts could offer a safe place for sexual services to be voluntarily traded, and that this combination of tolerance and realism is the best way to stop unwilling victims being coerced into the sex trade. Unfortunately, that is theory, not reality. We were not willing – we were victims. And throughout those years in which we slaved, we saw more and more women being trafficked and forced, through violence, intimidation and fear, into the legal, licensed windows alongside us. Nor is this just anecdotal evidence: in 2011 – just over a year after we escaped from our prison – Holland's chief anti-trafficking prosecutor admitted publicly that the legalisation of prostitution had led to an increase, not a reduction, in the number of sex-trafficking victims.

And the reason is obvious: just look at the cobbled alleys of De Wallen, revisit the glass prisons Olivia and I slaved in on *Achterburgwaal* and *Stoofsteeg*. Observe the loverboys, the pimping gangs, the drug dealers; see how they control the streets, operating brazenly in full sight of the uniformed police officers speeding along on their mountain bikes. Now can you see? Where is the regulation, where is the proper and honest policing? It does not exist. Legalising prostitution has been an excuse for the city – its government and its law enforcement – to abandon any attempt to protect the women who work in the Red Light District, whilst at the same time gratefully profiting from the tourist traffic flowing into it. To Olivia and I, this seems utterly and cynically wrong.

We have earned a say in this. Just as Richard Korver told us when we prepared for the court case against Ricardo, it is time for our voices to be heard. We have direct experience of what it really costs to sell sex; we know – we can testify to – the unalterable fact that it will permanently hurt any woman who does so. The girl who enters the windows of the Red Light District cannot be the same woman when – if – she manages to escape. We are the living proof of this.

We were forced into the windows on our eighteenth birthdays – the exact moment when our law permits the exchange of sex for money. We were still much too immature to understand what this existence would demand of us, and far too young to have the strength to resist the man who put us there. Just as I recognise that prostitution – legalised or otherwise – will always exist, I am absolutely certain that the age limit must be raised: twenty-five years of age should be the youngest age at which anyone should be paid for being penetrated.

Our ordeal was not unique in the years we worked in the Red Light District. It is not unique now. Every day and night, girls barely out of adolescence are repeatedly raped to satisfy the desires of men with more money than conscience, and the greed of exploiters who live off their suffering.

Who are these girls? They are someone's daughters, someone's sisters, or your children. Or a young girl you know. In the end we were lucky – we had each other.

We wrote this book for today's Anna and Olivia, because we know how easy it is for vulnerable young girls – those whose families or background leave them ripe for exploitation – to become ensnared in the commercial sex trade, and how difficult it is to get out.

We know too that parts of our story will have shocked – perhaps even sickened – you. I can't apologise for this: only by showing the terrible, lasting damage of renting our bodies can we sound a sufficiently loud alarm. Because above all we hope that telling our story will save some young girl like us from all that we suffered.

Thank you for listening. It is all we can ask.

Afterword

We understand that our story is so extreme that some readers may be tempted to dismiss it as either fantasy or exaggeration. Beyond them we know there are others – some of whom have an interest in the business of prostitution – who use social media to attack any survivors of the sex trade who dare to publish books about their ordeals.

But the rulings of the two courts which considered our case explicitly confirm everything we have written in this book. We have placed these legal documents – lightly edited for context and with redactions to protect real names – on our publisher's website and would urge anyone interested to read them.

www.orionbooks.co.uk/bodyforrent